The MUMS' Book

To Jacey,

Congratulations! I know you will be a fabulous and fun mum!
I'l babysit any time, just send me airfair!

love

Jess
x

xoxo

The MUMS' Book

FOR THE MUM WHO'S

Best AT Everything

ALISON MALONEY

Michael O'Mara Books Limited

First published in Great Britain in 2007 by
Michael O'Mara Books Limited
9 Lion Yard, Tremadoc Road
London SW4 7NQ

A CIP catalogue record for this book is available from the British Library

ISBN 978-1-84317-246-8

7   9   10   8

www.mombooks.com

Illustrations on pages 17, 18, 19, 20, 23, 26, 27, 28, 33, 72, 82, 98, 99,
100 (top and middle) © David Woodroffe 2007

Images on pages 35, 43 © Getty Images;
38, 41 © Mary Evans Picture Library; 13, 16, 60, 65, 66, 69, 73, 77 (bottom),
84, 90, 92, 93, 108, 109, 110, 111, 112, 114, 115 (top), 116, 117, 126, 131,
133, 134, 148, 150, 153, 158, 159 © Images courtesy of retroclipart.com

Cover design by Angie Allison from an original design
by www.blacksheep-uk.com

Designed and typeset by Martin Bristow

Printed and bound in England by Clays Ltd, St Ives plc

Disclaimer: Even the best mums need to make sure that their
children are always closely supervised when engaged in any of the
practical activities mentioned in this book.

To my Mum,
the best in the world

Contents

Introduction 9

Things You'll Never Hear a Mother Say
to Her Child 11

Party Time 13

Heroic Mums 35

Mother Nature: Sinners and Saints 46

Instant Tea Party 52

Clichéd Clashes 59

To Hell with Housework 60

The Wake-Up Call 65

Lights Out 67

Curing the Heebie-Jeebies 69

Kids' Kitchen 71

A Mother's Wisdom 83

Mum's the Word 87

'Me Time' For Mums: Perfect Pampering 89

Things My Mother Taught Me 93

Halloween Queen 95

Record-Breaking Mums 108

You're Not Going Out Dressed Like That! 112

CONTENTS

Oh, Mum!   114

Rainy Day Play   116

Outdoor Fun with the Kids   120

Are We Nearly There Yet?   126

'Me Time' For Mums: Let's Party!   130

Teen Trouble   133

Mum's Gone Shopping   140

Movie Mums From Hell   149

Other Mums' Books   155

Things You Wish Your Mother Had Told You   157

The Joke's On Mum   159

Introduction

Nobody knows how to do everything quite as well as a Mum does. From nursing scraped knees to mending broken hearts, Mum has a practical solution for every crisis and always keeps her head.

Who else could spend all day working, cleaning and shopping, and *still* turn up on time in the playground with a smile and a welcoming hug? Who else could manage to juggle career commitments alongside fulfilling the demands of a busy home life, and *still* have time to organize lifts to parties and family outings?

Nothing fazes the Mum who's best at everything. If there are six more kids than expected for tea, she'll whip up a wonderful pasta or produce some filling, tasty dish in minutes. If the children have left paint marks all over the carpet, she'll do a

'quick' steam-clean without smudging her make-up or getting a hair out of place. And she *never* loses her temper. Her house is always cosy and welcoming, and when other children go round to tea they are fed healthy, nutritious meals that they actually eat!

But, perfect as you are, everybody needs a little helping hand occasionally. Here you can learn how to throw the perfect party, how to spend fun-packed afternoons with your kids, and, best of all, how to make the most of your child-free time.

Share some stories about great mums, pushy mums and downright awful mums, and celebrate the multifaceted existence that we call motherhood.

Finally, just remember that to your own kids you will always be the *Mum who's best at everything.*

> *A mother's job is to be there when her children need her, but to bring them up so that they don't.*
> ***Author unknown***

Things You'll Never Hear A Mother Say To Her Child

Be good and I'll buy you a motorcycle!

✽

How on earth can you see the TV sitting so far back?

✽

Don't bother wearing a jacket – it's quite warm out.

✽

Let me smell that shirt.
Yes, that's good for another week.

✽

I think an untidy bedroom is a sign of creativity.

✽

Yes, I used to play truant, too.

Just leave all the lights on.
It makes the house more cheery.

✳

Could you turn the music up louder
so I can enjoy it, too?

Run and bring me the scissors! Hurry!

✳

Just turn your underpants inside out.
No one will ever know.

✳

No, I don't have a tissue with me –
just use your sleeve.

Party Time

Birthdays used to mean jelly and ice cream at home, a game of pass the parcel and a slice of birthday cake, but nowadays kids want nothing less than a full-scale disco or an outing to the cinema with twenty-five friends. It can get incredibly expensive, not to mention increasingly competitive, so how about going back to basics and entertaining the kids at home? If you can face the inevitable mess and cope with the occasional spillage, you can still throw the best party in the world in your own living room.

THE THEME'S THE THING

All the best parties have themes. Whether it's pirates, fairies or Harry Potter, make sure it is reflected in every aspect of the event, and not just the costumes. Below are a few suggestions, but as every child has different interests, you might want to organize the theme around a favourite programme or film instead.

SWASHBUCKLING PIRATES PARTY

Costumes: Pirate clothes are relatively simple and don't have to cost a fortune. All you need is a big, baggy shirt tied around the waist with a sash (perhaps made out of a long winter scarf or a

lengthy strip of plain material) and a baggy
pair of trousers, or an old pair of trousers
ripped, in raggedy lines, around the knee
and a striped T-shirt. Tie a scarf around the
head, add an eye patch and a toy sword,
and you have your very own Captain Jack.

Decorations: Fill the house with Jolly
Roger flags. If you're lucky you might be
able to find balloons with the skull and
crossbones as well but, if not, black and red
ones look equally good. Treasure maps also
make effective decorations.

   If you are having the party outside, build a pirate ship using
wooden pallets as decking. Then add bamboo sticks with old
sheets as sails, a Jolly Roger flag and a treasure chest made from
an old box, painted gold. If you have any old jewellery around,
add that for effect.

Food: Cut sandwiches into interesting shapes. Hands
(signifying the one that Captain Hook lost to a crocodile in
Peter Pan), treasure chests, boats and sails are all possibilities.

   If you are keen on baking, try making a pirate ship (see
recipe on page 18) or a simple cake with a skull and crossbones
decoration. A treasure chest cake is quite simple and can be
filled with sweets or chocolate coins, and it also looks fab (see
recipe on page 16). If you are not so great in the kitchen, it is

perfectly acceptable to buy a birthday cake, and there are plenty of pirate cakes in the shops.

Activities: Lay a treasure hunt in the house or, if the weather is nice, in the garden. Hide or bury a box or chest full of chocolate coins, and place clues all over the house to lead the children to it. TIP: When writing the clues, you'll find it's a lot easier to start at the point where you've hidden the treasure and work backwards.

Get the children to decorate some biscuits with pirate faces. Mix some icing sugar with a little water so that it can be spread on a round digestive or rich tea biscuit. Then provide hundreds and thousands, fruit decorations and sweets to make the features. You may want to use melted chocolate or coloured icing for an eye patch.

Games: Play 'Pin the Tail on the Parrot'. Draw or photocopy a large picture of a pirate with a parrot on his shoulder, or just the parrot itself. Then draw and cut out a tail and push a drawing pin through it. If you have a cork noticeboard, you can use that as the pin board. If not, a large piece of thick cardboard will do. Blindfold the children and ask them to pin the tail on the picture of the parrot. Kids find this hilarious! But make sure they take care when they're using those pins.

PIRATE-THEMED RECIPES

Treasure Chest Cake

Ingredients for cake mixture:
185 g (6.5 oz) butter
385 g (13.5 oz) caster sugar
3 eggs, beaten
300 g (10.5 oz) self-raising flour
70 g (2.5 oz) cocoa powder
1 cup of water

Ingredients for decoration:
75 g (3 oz) soft butter
120 g (4 oz) icing sugar
50 g (1.75 oz) cocoa powder
60 ml (2 fl oz) milk
silver/gold cake decorations

1 Grease a 19 cm- (7.5 inch-) square cake tin and line with baking paper.

2 Mix the butter, caster sugar, eggs, flour, cocoa powder and water in a large bowl with an electric mixer, or by hand, until the mixture is smooth.

③ Pour the mixture into the cake tin and bake for one and a half hours at 180°C (Gas mark 4 or 350°F). When baked, leave to stand for five minutes and then turn the cake on to a wire rack.

④ When the cake is cool, cut a 13 cm (5 inch) square from the centre of the cake to about half the depth. (The kids will love eating this bit while you cook!) Mix the icing sugar, cocoa powder, butter and milk, and then ice the remaining cake.

⑤ Create the illusion of metal studs on the outside of the chest with blobs of white icing or with silver or gold cake decorations. Then fill the centre with gold coins and sweets.

Now, as always, the most automated appliance in a household is the mother.
Beverly Jones

Pirate Ship Cake

*2 baked 23 cm- or 25.5 cm- (9 inch- or 10 inch-)
round cakes (using the Treasure Chest Cake recipe)*

Ingredients for decoration:
*4 cups chocolate butter icing
(see previous recipe)
1 packet Rolos (in foil wrappers)
1 packet Maltesers
1 KitKat finger
wooden cocktails sticks and/or wooden skewers
wafer rolls (or Coco Pops Straws)
paper sails (with skull and crossbones
either drawn or printed from a computer design)*

1 Cut the cakes in half, to make semi-circles. Stack each semi-circle on top of one another, to create a half-barrel shape, and attach them more firmly by spreading a thin coat of chocolate icing in between each layer.

2 Slice off the bottom curve to make the 'ship' sit better, then turn it upright, with the longer side on top. For extra safety, you can push cocktail sticks or drinking straws through the cake to help the halves stick together better.

3 Chill the cake in the fridge, then cover with the butter icing, placing a KitKat finger at one end of the 'ship' to make a 'plank'. Chill for another hour to firm the icing.

4 Place the wafer rolls or Coco Pops Straws around the edge of the 'deck' for a rope effect. Then add a pile of Maltesers for cannonballs and Rolos (still wrapped in their gold foil) for barrels. Stick the sails on to the skewers (if you have them) or on to the cocktail sticks.

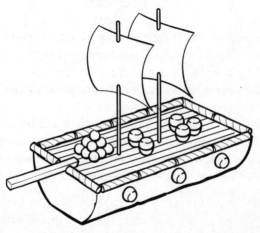

5 For the cannons, place three unwrapped Rolos on each side of the ship, held on with cocktail sticks. The birthday candles can be placed in the Rolos, or put on the deck.

FANTASTICAL FAIRIES PARTY

Costumes: Think pink. Most young girls have fairy dresses these days, but otherwise a leotard and cheap net tutu are ideal. Wings are inexpensive to buy, but should you want to make your own, you will need strong but pliable wire (the strength of coat-hanger wire), some netting or old white tights (if you have such things), and some elastic.

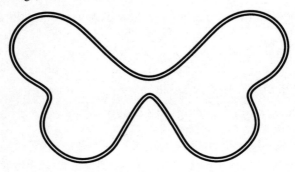

Bend the wire into the shape of butterfly wings and then cut out the material, using the wire as a template, but making it slightly larger so that it can be attached to the wire more securely. Then spread glue on the wire and stick the material to it carefully. When it is dry you can attach some sequins or use glitter paint on the wings to give them that extra sparkle. To make this essential accessory wearable, tie a piece of elastic around the centre of the wings, making two loops to go over your child's arms.

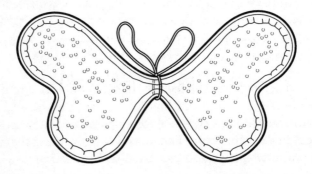

To make a wand, simply cut out a star from card and paint it with glitter paint, or cover in tin foil. Then stick it to the end of a long thin stick, or a pretty pencil.

Decorations: If you are having the party outside, decorate the garden with wind chimes, and perhaps even fairy lights (unless it's a bright, sunny day). Give the kids lots of bubble mixture, as bubbles flying around the garden will give it an enchanted look. Tie silver stars made out of card and tin foil to the branches of the trees and add strings of beads, such as the ones used to decorate Christmas trees.

A Wendy house can be transformed into a fairy grotto with colourful crêpe paper and fairy lights. If it's a winter party, put the fairy lights inside and decorate the walls with pink crêpe paper and silver stars. Sprinkle the party table with tiny glittery stars or hearts.

Food: Bake some biscuits in the shape of hearts and stars, or use a pastry cutter to cut the sandwiches in these special shapes. Fairy cakes are a must, of course (see page 76), and if you want to make them into butterfly cakes, slice a 2 cm (0.8 inch) circle from the centre and cut in half, then put some butter icing in the middle and stick in the two semi-circles so they look like wings.

Activities: Hide gold and silver chocolate coins and rainbow-coloured sweets around the house or garden, and give each child a 'fairy cup'. Then get them to look for as many treats as possible to put in their fairy cups. Encourage them by telling them they are 'warm' when near a treasure and 'cold' when far away.

Games: We've all played Musical Chairs, but with a lot of children it is difficult to manage this at home, so Musical Cushions is a great alternative for any party. Scatter enough cushions for each child and get them to sit down when the music stops. Then take one away for each turn and the child who fails to sit down on a cushion is out.

Pass the Parcel is an old favourite, but try special fairy wrapping paper or use crêpe paper in the colours of the rainbow (in the correct order, of course). You could also sprinkle some special 'fairy dust' i.e. glitter, inside each layer of wrapping paper (but not if you don't want to be hoovering it up for the next fortnight!).

PETER PAN AND FRIENDS PARTY

This is a great one for both boys and girls as they can all identify with characters in the classic story.

Costumes: There are a variety of different costumes to choose from and most are easy to make. Pirates and fairies, as above, can become Smee, Captain Hook (with the aid of a plastic hook and a floppy hat) and Tinker Bell. Anyone going as Wendy really needs nothing more than a long nightdress. Tiger Lily will need a long brown tunic, cut to a fringe around the bottom, and decorated with a beaded belt. Long hair should be tied into two plaits either side of the face and worn with thick, colourful hairbands. A headdress can be made from a ring of card, coloured in mosaic style, with a feather or two sticking straight up at the back.

Peter Pan's costume is probably the most difficult, but here is a simple way to make an excellent outfit. You will need some green felt, fabric scissors, fabric glue, a red feather, a large green T-shirt (preferably old or very cheap), some green tights, a belt and a toy sword (or you can make your own).

1 Estimate the size of your child's head using a tape measure. Then draw a triangle on a piece of green felt, with the triangle base measuring the same as the circumference of your child's head, and the height equalling about half the length of the base.

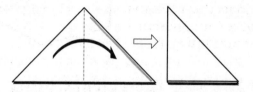

2 Cut out the triangle and fold it in half lengthwise. Glue the side edges together, leaving a tiny hole at the top.

3 Using a little glue, stick the feather into the hole.

4. Cut a jagged pattern along the bottom of the T-shirt and along the bottom of each sleeve.

5. Once 'Peter' has put on the customized T-shirt and the green tights, fasten the belt over the T-shirt, and add the fake sword (if you make it yourself, draw an outline of a sword on some scrap cardboard – the sturdier the better – cut it out, and perhaps cover it with tin foil).

6. For the finishing touch, add the hat – making sure the glue is completely dry first, otherwise your Peter Pan may suffer premature hair loss!

Decorations: Turn the house or garden into Neverland. You could transform a Wendy house into the Lost Boys' lair, or you could use pop-up tunnels and tents. If you have a small tent or a teepee, put that up for the Red Indian camp. A ball pool is a great alternative to using a paddling pool for the lagoon (and less messy too!). If the party is taking place inside, decorate the room with pirate flags and green crêpe paper.

Mermaids' Lagoon can be created with strips of blue and green crêpe paper mixed with strips of silver foil hanging down from walls or ceilings. Make a big moon, covered in foil, and cut out the shape of a pirate ship from black paper. Put the two together to make a simple, but very effective, decoration. Don't forget the stars, especially the second star on the right!

Food: Make a pirate cake (as shown on page 18), and cut sandwiches in the shape of Peter's hat, swords, the moon and stars.

Activities: Hide treasure at 'Hangman's Cove' where Captain Hook kept all his riches. Create a cave-like atmosphere in a wardrobe or in a cupboard under the stairs, and hide a chest of gold coins there, then tell the kids to start hunting.

Games: *Hide from the Pirates*. Outside, on the patio area or concrete floor, use chalk to draw circles, totalling one less than the number of kids present. Get the children to move around in different ways (e.g. hop, run, walk, fly like Tinker Bell, walk like the Indians). Occasionally, call out 'Hide from the Pirates!', which is the children's cue to scramble to find a 'hole'. The child who does not reach one in time has to stand in a 'hole' for the rest of the game. The contest continues until the last one to jump into the last 'hole' wins the game.

Whose Shadow? In a darkened room with curtains closed, suspend a white sheet from the top of the lintel in the doorway, making sure that the sheet reaches the floor. Split the kids into two teams, one on either side of the doorway. The team of kids in the room then take it in turns to walk closely past the sheet, using a torch to cast their shadow on it. The other team then has to guess whose shadow is walking by each time. The team with the most correct guesses wins.

FAIRY-TALE FUN PARTY

This theme appeals particularly to girls, as many fairy-tale characters are princesses, but boys are certainly not excluded with so many princes and knights to choose from.

Costume: Any princess dress will do, although there are other alternatives. How about making a simple red cape for Red

Riding Hood (see below) or adapting a raggedy dress for Cinderella (before her Prince Charming encounter)? Boys can go as knights, in a simple white tunic (a long T-shirt) with a shield or a cross drawn on it, carrying a sword and a shield. Glittery black tights make great chainmail trousers (if you can persuade your little knight to wear them) and, if you don't have a plastic helmet, make a cardboard crown and cover with gold paint or silver foil.

To make Red Riding Hood's cape and hood you will need two pieces of red felt or fleece, the first measuring 2 × 1 metres (79 × 39.5 inches) and the second measuring 1 × 0.5 metres (39.5 × 19.75 inches). (These are just estimates. It might be an idea to do the measuring *before* buying the cloth to make sure you have enough.)

1 Measure from the back of your child's neck down to their knee to determine the length of the cape. Fold the first piece of fabric in half to make a square and, using chalk or a pen, mark the length measurement down the crease, and also from left to right on the top edge of the fabric. Draw a curve between the two points to make a quarter-circle and cut along the curve through the double thickness of the fold to produce a semi-circle. Cut out a rounded neckline in the middle of the semi-circle.

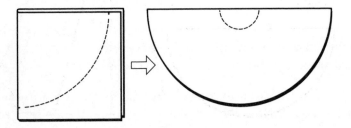

2 To make the hood you will need to cut out another semi-circle. To judge its size, first measure from your child's eyebrows across the top of the head and down to the base of the neck. Add 8 cm (3 inches) to this measurement and this will give you the radius of your semi-circle. Fold the fabric in half to make a square and, as above, mark the radius measurement down the crease, and also from left to right on the top edge of the fabric. Draw a curve between the two points to make a quarter-circle, and cut along it to produce a semi-circle.

After you have cut out the hood shape, remember that it is the straight edge that will be framing your face. You need to gather up the curved edge and then sew it to the rounded neckline of the cape.

3 Cut thin vertical slits just below the neckline of the main cape and thread a long red ribbon through, leaving plenty to use as a tie.

Decorations: Cover the house with sumptuous colours and fabrics. If you have any velvet, fake fur or gold fabric, drape it over chairs to create a regal look. If not, cover the chairs with red or purple crêpe paper or gold wrapping paper. Hang a foil curtain at the door of the party room and create the feeling of a ball, with dim lighting and silver foil and crêpe paper streamers. Make a throne for the birthday girl by putting a cushion on a dining-room chair and decorating the back with pink and purple strips.

Food: Make a princess cake – it's easier than it sounds! Use a metal pudding basin to bake a normal sponge cake (either from scratch – see Treasure Chest Cake recipe on page 16 – or from a shop-bought mixture if you want to save time). Leave the freshly baked cake to cool, then turn it upside down on to a plate. Stick a Barbie-type doll (preferably with the top half clothed!) into the baked cake, so that the cake becomes her skirt. If need be, scoop a little bit of the cake out to make way for her legs – a good excuse to be the first to taste it! Then decorate the skirt with icing and cake decorations however you wish. It may be advisable to bake another 23 cm- (9 inch-) flat sponge to add a little more depth in case your pudding basin isn't deep enough for the doll's impossibly long legs!

There are plenty of princess-themed biscuits and cakes out there for the party food, but you could also try heart- and star-shaped sandwiches, royal strawberries (strawberries dipped in chocolate) and pink drinks (fruit squash). Medieval chicken (roasted chicken legs) is usually quite popular too.

Activities: Let the children make their own crowns and conical princess hats. Cut out the shapes of crowns and the cone hats before the children arrive, and provide paint, glitter and stick-on gems for them to use. Obviously this can be very messy! The boys can also make shields and swords using cardboard, paint and tin foil. Alternatively, if it's a girl's party, buy a cheap bracelet-making kit, or just some beads and thin elastic, and let them make their own jewellery. This activity can keep kids happily occupied for ages and they also get to take their little work of art home at the end of the party.

Games: *Princess and the Pea – Mark 1.* Start this game by telling the story of 'The Princess and the Pea'. Then, invite the girls to have a go at detecting their own 'pea'. Arrange four pillows in a row on the floor and place a small ball under one of them. Each girl must sit on the pillows in turn, and guess which one the ball is under. Move the ball every time, and if you should you want to make it even more difficult, use a marble.

Princess and the Pea – Mark 2. Fill a jam jar with dried peas, counting them as you go. The children each guess how many peas they think are in the jar, and the winner gets a small prize.

The Queen Says . . . This game is simply the royal version of 'Simon Says . . .'.

Stick the Kiss on the Frog. This game is played just like 'Pin the Tail on the Donkey'. Enlist the help of someone artistic to

draw you a large frog on a piece of paper or card and attach it to an easel or to a wall. Then draw and cut out several pairs of red lips using paper or card and write the names of the guests on them. Add Blu Tack to the other side of the lips. Use a purple satin sash for the blindfold. Each child has a go at sticking their set of lips onto the frog and the winner is the one who sticks theirs closest to the mouth of the frog.

PYJAMA PARTY

This type of party is perfect for older children who may be past the 'dressing-up stage' but still love the excitement of a sleepover.

Costumes: Pyjamas (so that bit is nice and easy!).

Accessories: Tell everybody to bring their own sleeping bags and pillows, but make sure you borrow a couple of spares just in case.

Food: As a special treat, prepare a 'Midnight feast', although you don't have to wait until the middle of the night to give it to them. The best feasts are eaten in bedrooms, so make sure that what you provide isn't going to result in endless hours of cleaning. Peanuts are always a bad idea, as they tend to get thrown around by over-exuberant children, and will keep turning up in strange places for weeks. Non-messy sandwiches, like ham or cheese, are best, and wraps can be good if they are tightly curled and held together with a cocktail stick.

Games: *Chinese Whispers.* In this game a message is whispered into the ear of one child and must be carried by whispers along the line of children to see how well it travels. Some of the resulting sentences can be hilarious. To start off the rumours, you could cut out newspaper headlines and substitute real names with those of the guests. But keep the sentences silly, and avoid anything that might be true, insulting or embarrassing.

Quick on the Draw. This game is always a huge hit: Write down words, phrases and names of books, films, etc. on slips of paper and put them in a large bowl. Then divide the children into two teams and give each a pad of plain paper and a pencil. One member of each team has two minutes to draw as many of the phrases as possible and his or her team must guess each one before moving on to the next. No words or numbers can be written down and the child who is drawing must not speak or gesture. The team with the most points wins.

> *If evolution really works, how come mothers only have two hands?*
> ***Milton Berle***

OTHER POSSIBLE PARTY THEMES

＊ The Circus

＊ The Wizard of Oz

＊ Disney characters

＊ The Wild West

＊ Superheroes

＊ Harry Potter

GENERAL PARTY GAMES FOR YOUNGER CHILDREN

Switch!

Divide the children into two teams and take the first group into another room. Then get them to switch items of clothing, such as belts, shoes, sweaters and socks, and come back into the room. The other team must guess who has changed which items of clothing. You will need to keep a note of who is wearing what so that you can keep track of the scores. Make sure there are the same amount of switches for each turn, as the team who guesses the most is the winner. If the children are not wearing enough accessories or easily swappable clothing, get them to dress up first.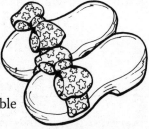

Puzzle Hunt

Take six different coloured pieces of paper and on each one draw a figure, such as a clown or a pirate, depending on the theme of the party. It could also be an animal such as a frog, a dog or a fish, as long as they can be separated into six identifiable pieces. Cut around the outline of your character and then divide into six pieces – for example, head, body, two legs and two arms. Number them 1 to 6. Then, using Blu Tack, stick the 36 separate pieces around the house or garden. Divide the children into six teams and give them each a colour to find. The first team to return with all six pieces of the puzzle, and to put the character together, is the winner.

Pass the Balloon

Get the children to sit in a circle and give one child a balloon. If there are lots of children, two balloons may be used. Put some music on. The children must pass the balloon around as quickly as they can. Whoever is holding it when the music stops is out. A ball can also be used. The last child left is the winner.

FOR OLDER CHILDREN

The Name Game

A similar game to 'Quick on the Draw', but for the less artistic. On separate scraps of paper, write down the names of as many famous people as you can, making sure they are people whom the children will know well, and then put the paper in a bowl. A mixture of fictional characters, such as Bart Simpson, and real celebrities, such as David Beckham, usually works well. Then one member of each team has two minutes to describe as many famous people as possible to his/her team members without mentioning the name on the paper or using a 'sounds like' clue. Their team gets a point for each person they name correctly, and after each team member has had their turn, the team with the most points is the winner.

Truth or Consequences

Write questions for the children on slips of paper and put them in a bowl. They can be slightly personal, such as 'Who is your boyfriend?' mixed with quiz questions such as 'What's the capital of France?' or 'What is $12 + 6$?' In another bowl, place slips of paper with forfeits for refusing to answer a question, telling a lie or getting it wrong. Make them fun, but not too embarrassing or scary. For example 'Hop on one leg while singing "Twinkle Twinkle Little Star"' or 'Walk around the room as if you were a gorilla.' It's an old favourite, but the results can be hilarious.

Mystery Melodies

Before the party, record a few bars of your child's favourite pop songs with thirty-second gaps between each. When all the children are there, play a few notes at a time, the first child to guess the song (and the artist, if you want to make it harder) gets a point. If nobody guesses it the first time, play a little more of the song until they do.

Heroic Mums

Most mums will say they would do anything for their children, but rarely is this put to the test. Here we pay tribute to those mothers who went the extra mile out of love, bravery or just plain silliness.

Agrippina (AD 15–59)

Agrippina the Younger was the most scheming of mothers, but her dubious actions were all motivated by one thing – devotion to her son, Nero. Agrippina gave birth to Nero during her first marriage to her second cousin, Gnaeus. After another brief marriage she wed her uncle, the Roman Emperor Claudius, in AD 49. She immediately took control of the Roman legions and set about furthering the ambitions of her son.

After making false accusations against Silanus, who was betrothed to Claudius's daughter Octavia, she secured her stepdaughter as Nero's bride. Silanus committed suicide on the day the couple wed.

Finally, Agrippina persuaded Claudius to adopt Nero officially, making him first in line to the Imperial throne, above his own son. Claudius died in AD 54 after eating poisoned mushrooms. Unsurprisingly, Agrippina was the prime suspect.

At last Nero became Emperor. And what thanks did his devoted mother get? Absolutely none. Nero decided she was far too bossy for his liking, so he plotted to kill her. He made four attempts, including trying to drown her by putting a hole in a boat. But Agrippina was made of tough stuff and she swam to shore. Finally, in AD 59, Nero sent his soldiers to beat her to death.

Legend has it that she pointed to her womb and told her killers to harm her in the place where Nero's life had begun.

Eleanor of Aquitaine (*c.*1122–1204)

Known as 'The Grandmother of Europe', Eleanor of Aquitaine wielded huge political influence over the continent through her marriages, her children and the marriages of her daughters.

At fifteen the Duchess of Aquitaine was married to the French King, Louis VII. She bore him two daughters and was highly influential in state matters during her marriage to Louis. In 1147 she led a company of 300 women to the Second Crusade, alongside her husband and his army, to fight as well as tend the wounded. However, after Louis became jealous over her relationship with an uncle, their marriage was annulled in 1152.

Six weeks later, swamped by suitors, Eleanor married Henry of Normandy, soon to become King Henry II of England. Together they had three daughters and five sons, which was no mean feat for a woman in her thirties in the twelfth century.

In 1173, Henry's sons Henry, Richard (later King of England) and Geoffrey rebelled against their father and Eleanor took her children's side (as mothers are wont to do). Caught trying to flee the country, Eleanor was imprisoned for fifteen years for her trouble and was only freed on her husband's death in 1189. On her release she granted amnesty to prisoners and ensured the loyalty of the English to her son, King Richard I, the Lionheart. When he was captured and imprisoned in Europe, she raised the ransom and secured his release.

After making sure her daughters had married worthy European rulers, Eleanor's attention turned to Richard's nuptials, and in 1191 she made an epic journey across the Pyrenees to escort Berengaria of Navarre to Cyprus for her marriage to the English king.

Eleanor died at the grand old age of eighty, and shortly before her death she successfully defended the territory of Anjou against her grandson, Arthur of Brittany.

Louise of Savoie (1476–1531)

Louise of Savoie was the mother of sixteenth-century French King François I. An interfering old bat at the best of times, she ruled the country while her warmonger son was fighting in Italy, and again when he was captured and imprisoned by the Holy Roman Emperor, Charles V.

She came into her own after François (who probably goes down in history as the most selfish father that ever lived), on his defeat and capture in Italy signed a treaty whereby he gave up certain territories and then secured his own freedom in exchange for that of his two young sons, François and Henri, who were eight and six. As if that wasn't bad enough, he left them to rot in a Spanish jail for three years while he merrily broke the treaty, ensuring that they would not be released.

While it is true that Louise had a hand in the incarceration of her poor motherless grandchildren, she was also instrumental in their release. After discovering that their conditions were not as luxurious as they should be, and that the King and Charles V had reached stalemate, she employed a dose of girl power.

She and daughter Marguerite approached the Emperor's aunt and sister. If the men were too stubborn to budge, she reasoned, the women would have to sort out the mess. The four met at Cambrai, northern France, on 5 July 1529, where they took a month to negotiate a treaty to end the war and ensure the safe return of her grandchildren.

The resulting agreement was considered so fair and sensible that even the troublesome men couldn't find fault with it. Happily they signed the Treaty of Cambrai, which became known as 'La Paix des Dames' or 'The Peace of the Ladies'.

Isabella Beeton (1836–65)

Otherwise known as Mrs Beeton, Isabella was born in London in March 1836 and, during her short life, her domestic juggling act would have put Nigella Lawson to shame.

She had a difficult time during and after the birth of her children. Her first child died young and after the tragedy she immediately returned to work at her husband's publishing firm. A second child also died and a third became very ill, at which point she and her husband moved to the Thames Valley. There she worked right up until the birth of her fourth child, as the family were in desperate need of the money. Returning to work too soon after the baby was born affected her health and she died from puerperal fever at the tender age of twenty-eight.

During her short and tragic life, however, she managed to work, bring up children and run a soup kitchen from her home for the poor children of Hatch End in London.

Oh, and she became the cookery star of her time with *Mrs Beeton's Book of Household Management,* which contained hundreds of recipes as well as useful tips for running the house. Published in 1861, it remains one of the best practical guides ever written.

Brave Bolivian Mothers

On 27 May 1812, the Spanish royalist army approached the beautiful Bolivian city of Cochabamba. The townspeople had been urged to resist the onslaught but, following a devastating war of independence, there were few grown men left to take up arms. Instead, a group of women on the outskirts of the town heroically fought and died alongside their children.

Their leader was Manuela Eras de Gandarillas, an almost blind mother in her sixties, who, two years earlier, had watched royalist forces execute her much-loved brother, José Domingo. Sadly, the women's rudimentary weapons and lack of strength in numbers meant defeat was inevitable.

Josephine Baker (1906–75)

The original Angelina Jolie, Baker adopted twelve children of varying ethnic backgrounds from around the world and called them her 'Rainbow Tribe'. Born Freda Josephine McDonald in the slums of St Louis, Missouri, she dropped out of school when she was twelve. In a time of apartheid in the USA, she overcame racial barriers to become one of the most versatile performers of her day. A star of stage and screen Josephine refused to play to segregated audiences and was instrumental in the integration of Las Vegas nightclubs.

Furthermore, she was decorated for her undercover work for the French Resistance during the Second World War and was the first American woman to receive French military honours at her Paris funeral.

Amy Hawkins

On 17 April 2006, a tornado ripped through Tennessee, claiming the lives of twelve residents. Amy Hawkins was at home with her two sons, six-year-old Jair and three-year-old Cole, and she ushered them down to the basement. As the tornado neared, she lay on top of her boys while the family home was ripped apart, acting as a shield from falling debris. The boys were fine, but their thirty-three-year-old mother was critically injured and was rushed to hospital where she underwent emergency surgery on her back, which had been crushed.

She is now paralysed from the hips down and has been told she will never walk again. In August 2006, her family home was rebuilt by the ABC show *Extreme Makeover* after public reaction to Amy's story made her a national celebrity.

> *When you are a mother, you are never really alone in your thoughts ... A mother always has to think twice: once of herself and once for her child.*
> **Sophia Loren**

While some mums are heroines, others let the side down. Here are some glimpses of motherhood gone wrong.

Jocasta, Queen of Thebes

According to Greek mythology, Jocasta had five children, the most famous being Oedipus, whom she ended up marrying.

When Oedipus was born, it was foretold that he would murder his father and marry his mother. So, in a pretty dumb attempt to avoid this fate, his father King Laius took the three-day-old baby, bound by the ankles, and left him to die on a 'barren, trackless mountain'. However, the king's servant was appalled by such a brutal act and duly rescued the tot, giving him to the childless King Polybus.

Fate took another twist when Oedipus, learning of his destiny, feared he would harm his family and so he ran away from them. At Thebes he unknowingly murdered his birth father and married his real mother, just as the oracle had predicted. Jocasta bore her son four children, but after learning of her unwitting incest, she committed suicide.

If only they'd kept him at home, none of this would have happened!

Agave

In Greek mythology Agave was the mother of Pentheus, King of Thebes. She was also a Maenad, a devoted follower of the god Dionysus. When her son refused to recognize Dionysus as the son of Zeus, he faced serious punishment for such a heinous crime.

In revenge, the angry god made the women of the court delusional. Agave saw her son, thought he was a beast, and along with other Maenads she helped to tear him to pieces.

Ma Barker (1873–1935)

Kate 'Ma' Barker was the matriarch of the notorious Karpis-Barker gang. During the era of the American Depression, she and her sons, Herman, Lloyd, Arthur, and Fred teamed up with criminal Alvin Karpis and several others and went on a four-year crime spree, which involved bank robberies, murders and kidnappings.

In 1933 the gang kidnapped millionaire William Hamm and received a ransom of $100,000. The following year, they abducted Minnesota banker Edward Bremer, Jr, whose ransom brought them $200,000. However, they met their match in Bremer's father, who was a good friend of President Franklin D. Roosevelt, and he determined to stamp out such illegal activities.

Soon after, FBI agents created highly skilled 'flying squads', which specialized in hunting down the leading criminals and public enemies of the day. Ma Barker was gunned down by a flying squad in 1935, along with her son Fred.

At the time of the gang's brutal spree, Ma Barker was seen as the mastermind behind her boys' crimes. This was later disputed by Alvin Karpis, who claimed that she merely provided the cover of a law-abiding widow travelling with her sons, but FBI chief J. Edgar Hoover believed she was as guilty as the men in every crime.

Calling her a 'veritable beast of prey', Hoover is quoted by Ken Jones in *The FBI in Action* (1957) as saying 'Ma Barker and her sons, and Alvin Karpis and his cronies, constituted the toughest gang of hoodlums the FBI ever has been called upon to eliminate.'

In 1977, she was immortalized in the Boney M hit 'Ma Baker', albeit with her name incorrectly spelled.

Mama Rose (1892–1954)

Gypsy Rose Lee's mother featured heavily in the musical *Gypsy*, but it seems her loyal daughter was really quite kind to her mama and glossed over certain aspects of the family history to hide the faults of her terrible parent.

The original pushy stage mother, Rose Thompson Hovick first abandoned baby Rose, leaving her with relatives while she took her toddler June to Hollywood to star in silent films. Her preferred technique for making her child cry for the camera was to tell June that their dog had died.

At the age of seven, little Rose was taken out of school to join her mother and sister, and she was taught to lie to truant officers if questioned. Mama Rose forced her daughters into vaudeville and threatened to give them away if they didn't do well. She trained them to steal from hotels and to leave restaurants before paying, and she once pushed a hotel manager out of a window.

Mama Rose even tried to shoot sixteen-year-old June's husband after having him arrested on false charges, but he escaped death only because when she pulled the trigger, the safety catch was still on. It was also rumoured that she shot her own boyfriend, although the official verdict was suicide.

Even when on her deathbed, legend has it that she was still having a dig at her daughters. Her last words to Gypsy Rose Lee were, allegedly, 'Wherever you go, I'll be right there. When you get your own private kick in the ass, just remember – it's a present from me to you.'

What a gem!

Joan Crawford (1905–77)

A Hollywood legend, and star of such classics as *Mildred Pierce* and *Whatever Happened to Baby Jane?*, she was an icon to a generation of moviegoers. But La Crawford wasn't always the nicest person off screen and, although she adopted five children, she was hardly a shining example of motherhood.

All of the children were bought from less than reputable

adoption agencies and one of the babies, a boy called Christopher whom she adopted in 1931, was taken away after his biological mother found out where he was and demanded him back. Despite being reunited with her son after wresting him back from Crawford, his mother would later sell him to another family.

Crawford's eldest daughter Christina, and her brother, who was also named Christopher, were disinherited by Joan on her death in 1977. Her will explained, simply '. . . for reasons which should be well known to them'. Christina, in return, wrote the bestselling book *Mommie Dearest*, detailing a life of abuse with her cruel, alcoholic adoptive mother who was more interested in her career than her children. In it she detailed the thrashings she received for using a wire coat hanger, as well as being 'harnessed' to her bed while her mother seduced her movie-star lovers downstairs.

One night Crawford brought Kirk Douglas home after a date and seduced him by dropping her dress as soon as they were in the house. After making love on the floor, Crawford went upstairs to check on the children. Douglas followed, and noticed the tots 'safely' strapped to their beds. 'I got out fast!' he recalled.

That's showbiz!

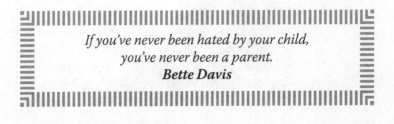

*If you've never been hated by your child,
you've never been a parent.*
Bette Davis

Mother Nature: Sinners and Saints

The maternal instinct is the most natural thing in the world. Our hormones ensure that in the vast majority of cases, we love each and every child we bring into the world, nurture them, and care for them in every way we can.

After all Nature is a mother, so all female animals have a maternal instinct, don't they? Well, although they may have some motherly love to give, it seems there are some terrible parents in the animal kingdom.

MOTHERS OF DUBIOUS CHARACTER

Pandas

The cute, cuddly image of this black-and-white bear is something of an illusion when it comes to looking after her young. How often have we celebrated the birth of a panda cub in a zoo and marvelled at the way the mother interacts with her offspring. The problem begins when the mother gives birth to twins – often she decides that one of the cubs is stronger and more likely to survive than the other, and then she completely abandons the weaker one! Mother love can certainly be tough.

Guinea Hens

The guinea hen is fantastically protective of her eggs and makes a nest off the ground to guard them and keep them warm until they hatch. But it's when her babies start to hatch that the problem starts. The mother hen is up at first light to gather bugs, and the tiny chicks (or 'keets'), inevitably try to follow their mum when she leaves the nest. As the nest is usually in a field, this invariably means trailing through long, often wet, grass. Unfortunately, Mum seems oblivious to the under-developed stature of her chicks, and she walks very fast, almost unaware that her babies are trying in vain to keep up. Although the mother's mission is clearly to find food for her brood, quite a few of the exhausted chicks often fall away and die in the grass, leaving her with far fewer babies to feed than before her food-finding travels.

Penguins

Often thought to be among the best parents in nature for the protective way in which they nurture the eggs, penguins also have a heartless streak. Royal penguins, for example, lay two eggs in a season, the second being 60 per cent larger than the first. Just before the second egg arrives, mum discards the first by rolling it out of the nest. Magellanic penguins hatch two eggs and the mother then gives 90 per cent of the fish she catches to one chick, ignoring the other's howls of hunger. The neglected chick invariably dies.

Rabbits

What could be cuter than tiny baby bunnies? How could rabbit mum resist? Well, in some cases, they can't resist . . . eating them. Some experts think this phenomenon is caused by stress, and will often happen with human interference; others believe it is because the doe simply doesn't understand what these small creatures are. Either way the result is not pretty!

African Black Eagles and Bald Eagles

The eagle can have two or three eaglets and will scour the countryside for food for her babies, often leaving dad in charge. On her return, however, she will allow the strongest one or two of her young to hog all the food and then simply stand by and watch the stronger eaglet or eaglets peck a weaker sibling to death.

Mice

Like the rabbit, first-time mums will sometimes eat their own litter due to confusion or stress. They may also kill one or two of the weaker babies, as surviving in the wild can be a difficult affair and a mummy mouse can't afford to nurture the ones that will straggle behind the rest. The solution does seem a bit drastic, though.

Tree Shrews

Tree shrews prefer to put their man before their babies. After giving birth, the female lives with her mate in one tree and leaves her babies in a nest some distance away. She visits the nest once every two days to give her young some milk.

NATURAL MOTHERS

Before you start to think that humans are the only creatures that really care about their babies, it's perhaps time to remind ourselves that there are loads of great mums in nature. Here are a few of the best.

Whales, Porpoises and Manatees

As they are mammals, these sea creatures nurse their young and keep them with them at all times throughout the nursing period. They also nudge them to the surface at regular intervals for air. The baby swims close to its mother and is carried in the

mother's 'slip stream' and she becomes extremely aggressive if her baby is threatened. Don't we all?

Elephants

Elephant calves are among the luckiest offspring in nature. Not only do they get a great mum, but a whole herd of great aunties as well who will all be present at the birth. In the first year, as they are small enough to be trampled under the feet of their elders, the calf is in constant contact with mum. If they stray over twenty yards away, they will be retrieved. Typical weaning takes four or five years, but the bond is not then broken. A nine-year-old elephant still spends half its time within five yards of its mum. Interestingly enough, the males move away, but the bond between mother and daughter lasts up to fifty years. Closely related females look after each other's calves, sometimes even suckling them, and a baby elephant will drink 11.3 litres of milk a day! Now *that's* devotion to the sisterhood.

Alligators

Although they are cold-blooded, alligator mums appear to have a warm heart. They lay between twenty and sixty eggs, which they bury in a nest mound and protect fiercely throughout the two-month incubation period. When the eggs are ready to hatch the mother digs into the nest mound, opens any eggs that have not hatched, and carries the young down to the water. Baby alligators stay close to their mum for the first two years, hibernating with her for the first year. During that time you don't want to go near – she will defend them to the death.

Kangaroos

As a marsupial, the kangaroo has a built-in baby carrier, so, immediately after birth, the lucky joey crawls up its mum's body and into a nice warm pouch. Inside, it attaches itself to one of four teats, which then enlarges to hold the joey in place. So, for the first few weeks it has food on tap and is constantly warm. After that, the joey will make occasional forays away from the pouch and will leave altogether after seven to ten months. While the males tend to go their own way when they are old enough, daughters stick close to mothers for several years.

> *As a parent you try to maintain a certain amount of control and so you have this tug-of-war ... You have to learn when to let go. And that's not easy.*
> **Aretha Franklin**

Instant Tea Party

(Or, how to throw a tea party for your seven-year-old and his/her five friends with only two hours' notice)

Turning up at the playground for the afternoon pick-up, your usual friendly smile turns into a frozen rictus grin as your child runs out with the five friends he or she has generously invited to tea without telling you. Meanwhile, their grateful mothers cheerfully wave their children goodbye (overjoyed to have some precious time to themselves), and arrange to pick them up later.

Of course, as a practised goddess, you will be able to mask the rising panic within as you mentally count the number of fish fingers you have left in the freezer and wonder how on earth you're going to get some more oven chips as hubby has the car and the nearest shop is four miles away.

After the initial fear of wondering how you'll cater for all the little darlings, it's not long before some common sense and a bit of clever thinking eventually kicks in. Pretty soon you're hosting the perfect instant tea party, and the children are eating out of your hands (not literally, I hope). Here's how you'll have done it.

1 **Distract the kids**

When friends are visiting, most kids are happy to run upstairs and put some serious effort into trashing the bedroom. If they, or you, are not thrilled with that idea, set up an art corner with pens, pencils and (if you can stand the mess) paints, and sit the children down. Give them a snack of cheese, fruit or yogurt first, so they don't whine about being hungry for the next hour or so.

2 **Forget the junk food and throw a party**

The kids may love chicken nuggets, but who can resist proper party fare? Finger food always goes down well, so here are a few suggestions for a quick and easy spread:

* Carrot and cucumber fingers

* Cheese straws

* Chicken legs

* Olives

* Cherry tomatoes

* Grapes

* Sliced apples

* Pizza (see recipes below)

* Potato wedges (see recipe below)

I know how to do anything – I'm a mom.
Roseanne Barr

Easy Pizza

Most children love pizza and it's so simple to make.

For the base:
75 ml (3 fl oz) lukewarm water from the tap
1 teaspoon sugar
1½ teaspoons dried yeast
225 g (8 oz) strong or plain flour
1 teaspoon salt
1 egg, beaten
½ teaspoon olive oil

For the topping:
375 g (13 oz) tin tomatoes, preferably chopped
tomato puree
cheddar or mozzarella cheese

1. Whisk the water and sugar in a basin, and add the yeast. Leave for 10–15 minutes until it is frothy.

2. Sift the flour and salt into a mixing bowl, then pour in the yeast and egg and a little water, if needed. Mix to a dough-like consistency and knead for 10 minutes on a board or work surface. Put the mixture back into the bowl and cover with cling film or a damp cloth, then leave for an hour.

3. Meanwhile, mix the chopped tomatoes with a teaspoonful of tomato puree. Then grate the cheddar or slice the mozzarella.

4 Place the dough in a shallow oblong baking tin (25×28 cm or 10×11 inches). Flatten and push out to the sides then brush with olive oil. Spread the tomato mixture on top, followed by the cheddar or mozzarella, and bake in the oven at 220°C (425°F or Gas mark 7) for 15–20 minutes.

Even Easier Pizza

This can be made with several types of breads that you may have in the house. Focaccia, ciabatta, and French bread work well, and so do pittas (especially mini ones) and even muffins or rolls. The long-life, half-baked variety is perfect.

1 Slice the bread lengthways (unless using pittas) and drizzle with a little olive oil.

2 Spread the tomato mixture (as above) on to the bready side, and top with ham, cooked bacon or cooked chicken (optional), then with cheese.

3 Bake in a hot oven at 240°C (475°F or Gas mark 9) until they are well warmed and the cheese has melted. The half-baked bread should bake for at least as long as the instructions require.

Healthy Potato Wedges

1 Cut the potatoes into large chunks and boil for ten minutes.

2 Drain and place on a baking tray.

3 Brush with oil and bake in the oven at 200°C (400°F or Gas mark 6) for 25 minutes. Serve with ketchup or mayonnaise.

Tasty Tomato Pasta

3 tbsp extra virgin olive oil
1 onion, finely chopped
2 garlic cloves, crushed
2 × 400 g (14 oz) cans chopped tomatoes
2 tsp sugar
1 large handful basil leaves, torn into pieces
salt and ground black pepper
155 g (5.5 oz) pasta shells (or any pasta
you have handy)
grated parmesan/Cheddar cheese, to serve

1 Heat the oil in a saucepan, add the onion and garlic, and gently fry until softened. Add some salt and pepper to season.

2 Stir in the tomatoes and sugar. Keep stirring occasionally and simmer on a low heat for 45–60 minutes.

3 Add the basil and season with salt and pepper. The sauce will be naturally chunky, but if you prefer a smoother consistency just put it in a blender for a few seconds.

4 Pour the sauce over your cooked pasta, and sprinkle grated cheese over the meal as required.

Chicken/Ham Wraps

1 Take a packet of tortilla wraps and spread a little mayonnaise on each.

2 Add shredded lettuce, grated cheese and cooked chicken or shredded ham, then roll into a wrap.

3 Alternatively, fill pitta breads with the same mixture and roll them tightly, securing with cocktail sticks at regular intervals. Then cut into bite-sized pieces.

SWEET TREATS

Before teatime, why not get the kids involved in making their own dessert? It needn't involve too much time or mess. Here are some simple recipes that the kids can help you with.

Easy Peasy Crispy Cakes

1 large bar milk chocolate
150 g (5.5 oz) rice crispies or cornflakes
12 paper bun cases
1 wooden spoon
1 small Pyrex or metal bowl

1 Put some water in the saucepan and bring to the boil.

Place 13 squares of chocolate into the bowl (you can eat the rest!) and carefully place the bowl into the saucepan.

2. Put the rice crispies or cornflakes into a very large mixing bowl (kids have a tendency to mix roughly and make a terrible mess!). Pour the melted chocolate over the cereal and mix thoroughly, until all the crispies/cornflakes are covered.

3. Spoon the chocolate-coated cereal into the paper cases and leave to set for 15 minutes.

Banana Brûlée

4 ripe bananas
400 ml (14 fl oz) Greek yogurt
2 tablespoons demerara sugar

1. Peel and thinly slice the bananas, and place into four ramekin dishes. Top with the Greek yogurt and sprinkle a layer of sugar on top.

2. Place under a heated grill until they are golden and bubbling. Leave them to cool, but do not put them in the fridge.

2. Enjoy!

Clichéd Clashes

(Or, things your children are bound to say, and your likely response)

But she started it!
I don't care who started it. *I'm* finishing it.

❋

I didn't do it!
Well, someone must have done.

❋

Why can't I have it?
Because money doesn't grow on trees.

❋

That's so unfair!
Life is unfair.

❋

Daddy said I could have it!
Then Daddy can pay for it.

❋

Johnny's mummy lets him do it!
Good for Johnny's mummy.

❋

Why?
Because I said so!

To Hell with Housework

10 EXCUSES NOT TO DO HOUSEWORK

1. According to the Royal Society for the Prevention of Accidents (RoSPA), in 2002 110,085 people were injured while cooking or cleaning in the UK alone – and those are just the ones who needed hospital treatment. At least sitting on the sofa with your feet up is unlikely to cause serious injury.

2. As soon as the kids get home, they'll mess it up anyway. As comedian Phyllis Diller put it so profoundly: 'Cleaning your house while your kids are still growing is like shovelling the [side]walk before it stops snowing.'

3. Wit and raconteur Quentin Crisp had the right idea when he said, 'There was no need to do any housework at all. After the first four years the dirt doesn't get any worse.'

4. Cleaners are very reasonable in price and it feels good to provide someone with employment. If you don't work and you can't bear the thought of watching someone else do your cleaning, grab some 'me time' and go shopping or have lunch with a friend while someone else slaves away amidst the dust and debris of your home.

5. You are unlikely to be appreciated for your effort, whereas a great new outfit

and a makeover will make you feel better and may impress the man in your life. As comedian Joan Rivers once said, 'Don't cook. Don't clean. No man will ever make love to a woman because she waxed the linoleum – "My God, the floor's immaculate. Lie down, you hot bitch."'

6 There's always tomorrow!

7 Make sure you have a friend who is messier than you. When you despair at the state of your house, pop round to visit her. You'll be amazed at how tidy your house seems when you get home.

8 If you have friends with immaculate houses, tell yourself that they must have too much time on their hands and lead a really boring life. You are *far* too interesting to spend all that time washing the windows, polishing the furniture, dusting the radiators, hoovering the curtains and scrubbing the kitchen floor.

9 Have you heard of *spring* cleaning? Once a year is enough.

10 Frankly, there's always something better to do!

> *My idea of superwoman*
> *is someone who scrubs her own floors.*
> **Bette Midler**

10 HOUSEWORK SHORTCUTS

1 If you have a dishwasher that gets sludgy and smelly, don't buy expensive cleaning products. Put a mug full of soda crystals in the bottom and set it to wash without any other crockery or cutlery inside.

2 Use a lint roller to dust the lampshades.

3 Use the vacuum cleaner with a brush attachment to dust everything. Not only is it quicker than a duster, it actually sucks up the dust rather than just displacing it.

4 Effervescent stomach tablets (e.g. Alka-Seltzer) make a great cleaner for stained vases and thermos flasks. Drop in a couple of tablets and leave to soak for an hour or so before rinsing out. They are also effective cleaners of jewellery. Put two tablets in a glass and then soak jewellery for two minutes.

5 Place a cup of ammonia in your oven overnight and wipe clean in the morning with a damp sponge. If you do this once a month you will never have the horrible job of scrubbing the baked on grease off the oven. It's worth the few minutes a month.

6. Use white vinegar to remove limescale in baths and also to get crayon marks off paintwork.

7. To keep lint and dust off glass-top tables, wash them in a solution of warm water and fabric softener, using one tablespoon of liquid fabric softener to one quart of warm water. The softener will clean the glass inexpensively and will help keep lint from gathering on the glass. This cleaning solution is also great for computer screens and TVs.

8. Got a young boy or two who can't quite hit the target when going to the loo? Put a ping-pong ball in the bowl and tell them to aim at it. Suddenly, peeing is fun – and much more accurate! Just make sure the ball doesn't get stuck or lost when you flush . . .

9. Bribe your kids to do the housework for you! If you have a daughter of the right age, tell her you are playing princesses and she is Cinderella. Then you can be the wicked Stepmother and she'll be mopping the kitchen floor in no time! If you have a boy and a girl, try the Hansel and Gretel story.

10. Don't try to brush pet hairs off your furniture. Just wipe the upholstery with a slightly dampened sponge.

GETTING THE KIDS TO DO SOME WORK

Children often need a little bribery to motivate them, so the best way of getting your housework done is to set them some tasks to earn their pocket money. It helps if you work out a 'fee' for each task. The table below is just an example; you may want to adjust the amounts to suit the age of your children.

✳ Emptying the dishwasher – 50p

✳ Mopping the floor – 50p

✳ Washing up – 50p

✳ Drying up – 50p

✳ Tidying a room – £1

✳ Dusting a room – £1

✳ Vacuuming a room – £1

✳ Washing the car – £2

✳ Tidying their own room – nothing!
They should do that anyway.

The Wake-Up Call

Before the kids were old enough to go to school, you did everything in your power to make them stay in bed longer in the morning. Remember those weekends when the kids would jump out of bed, full of beans at 6 a.m., and drag you kicking and screaming downstairs to make breakfast?

As soon as they go to school, everything changes! Try to get them up at 7 in the morning, and they pull the duvet over their heads and groan. No matter what you do, they refuse to budge, resulting in a huge last-minute rush and everybody being late for school.

So, to help you to avoid the pre-school panic, here are the ten best ways of getting your kids up in the morning.

1. Put your favourite Barry Manilow album in their CD player, and turn it up to full volume.

2. Threaten to dock their pocket money for every extra minute they don't budge.

3. Put a cold, wet flannel down the back of their pyjama top.

 Tell them their favourite programme is on TV – whether it's true or not.

 Tickle their feet.

6 Go out the front door and slam it loudly so they think you are leaving without them. (This only works with younger children. Teenagers merely breathe a sigh of relief and go back to sleep.)

7 Tell them there is only one portion of their favourite cereal left and that their little brother is about to eat it.

8 Start picking up their toys, computer games and favourite clothes from their floor and cupboards, and putting them in a black bin liner.

9 Tell them their Great-Aunt Nell is about to pop in – they'll be dressed and out the door in ten seconds flat!

10 Scream and point at the bottom of their bed, then, without any explanation, run out of the room. (Obviously this tactic only works occasionally, so it is only to be used in dire emergencies.)

Lights Out

Of course, the evening brings the opposite problem. You're shattered and can't wait to get the kids off to bed. They just want to finish their game or watch the end of a DVD and there's always something they just *have* to do before bedtime.

If bedtime is a battleground, here are the ten best ways of getting the children to bed.

1 Keep them away from the chocolate biscuits and fizzy drinks – or they'll be bouncing on the bed rather than sleeping in it!

2 Put on your best thespian tones and read them a bedtime story – but don't make it *too* exciting.

3 Make them run around the garden for several hours when they get home from school. That way, they'll be so tired that they'll crawl into bed early.

4 Milk and bananas are both supposed to aid sleep, so whip up a banana smoothie – but don't add sugar! Marmite also helps, but I wouldn't recommend adding that to the smoothie.

5 Lavender is great for making kids sleepy. Please don't make them eat it (it's disgusting!). Just add a drop of lavender oil to their bath instead.

6. Turn the TV off. There may be tantrums, but you must stand firm. This usually has them traipsing upstairs on time. It doesn't work, however, if they have a TV in their room, as they will simply carry on watching it there.

7. Alter the minute hand on the clock so that they think it's half an hour later than it is! This works a treat in the winter when it gets dark early.

8. As with the wake-up call, the threat of an elderly great-aunt popping round for tea should see them off.

9. Try a soothing CD in their player, if they have one in their room. Or a talking book, which can lull them to sleep.

10. Treat yourself to a glass of wine (or two) before the kids are in bed. It won't help them get to bed any quicker, but you won't care quite so much!

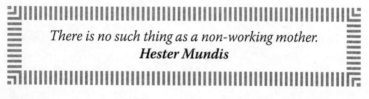

There is no such thing as a non-working mother.
Hester Mundis

Curing the Heebie-Jeebies

You've just dropped off to sleep when a wail that would frighten a banshee disturbs the peace. Chances are your child is not being attacked by an axe-wielding maniac, but is simply having a bad dream.

We can all remember waking up terrified of whatever has darkened our dreams, so the best thing to do is avoid storming into the room, screaming and shouting. Unless your child wakes you up every night with the same complaint, they may actually be genuinely frightened, so behaving like a monster can only make matters worse.

Try the following tips to sooth away those frightening childhood nightmares.

1. Make a hot, milky drink for your traumatized son or daughter. If you can be bothered traipsing downstairs to the kitchen, these usually work a treat.

2. Tell your child a nice, quiet story – but make sure it doesn't contain witches, vampires, ghosts or monsters!

3 Paint a relaxing scene in your child's mind. For example, tell them to imagine they are on a beach, with the waves lapping against the shore and that they are building sandcastles with their friends. Sound effects can help if you are any good at lapping waves!

4 Put a song in their head. Think of their favourite song and see if they can go over the lyrics – silently, of course. This is not such a great idea if their musical tastes happens to extend to thrash metal or gangsta rap.

5 Talk about your next holiday or day trip. Reminding them of something they are looking forward to can take their mind off whatever they have been dreaming about.

6 Stay with them for a while, stroking their hair or back, as this is very soothing.

7 Encourage them to tell you what was in the dream and suggest ways to overcome the thing that is frightening them. This can be done the following morning and may prevent recurring dreams.

8 Tell the children that whatever is in the dream can't hurt them and that you are there to protect them. Let them know it is safe to go back to sleep.

9 Switch on a nightlight if the dark is making them more afraid.

10 *Don't* take them into your own bed. This sends a subconscious message that their bed is frightening and yours is safe. You'll never get them to go back to their own bed again!

Kids' Kitchen

Children adore making things in the kitchen, and, if you teach them well, they can even be a help.

There are few things as wonderful as the first time your child brings you a cup of tea in bed. Then you know some of the hard work is over. Make sure you keep it safe, though, and always take the age of your child into consideration. After all, you don't want your four-year-old gamely trying to make you a cuppa!

Always supervise your children in the kitchen, especially when pots and pans are on the boil or something is in the oven, and keep the younger ones away from sharp knives.

Keep it fun, too, and don't get stressed if the cake mix gets smeared all over the counter or the dinner ends up on the floor! You can start with something easy, like the classic 'cress heads'.

Cress Heads

Although this activity doesn't involve cooking, making cress heads is one of the most fun and simple things to do in the kitchen. You'll need some empty, almost whole eggshells to start with. Carefully wash them out, then fill them with some damp cotton wool. Let the children draw funny faces on the shells (but tell them to be gentle, as cracked eggs will result in tears!).

Sprinkle some cress seeds on the cotton wool and wait for them to flourish. Cress seeds will grow almost anywhere,

but the best place to keep them is probably indoors on the windowsill where they will get most light. Encourage the children to keep the cotton wool damp by adding drops of water every day. After a few days, the funny faces will have spiky, edible green hair.

An extra tip: make sure the children know you want to eat the cress. They can always help by giving the cress heads a haircut themselves.

Toastie Teddies

Easy and fun, this is a great snack for the kids to make.

You will need:
4 slices bread
some olive oil
a teddy-shaped cookie cutter

1 Use the cutter to make teddy-bear shapes from the bread (the kids will love doing this bit!).

2 Brush the teddies with olive oil and place in the oven for 5–6 minutes on 180°C (350°F or Gas mark 4) until they are golden brown.

3 To serve, you can top them with just about anything: tuna, cheese, tomato, peanut butter or egg mayonnaise.

Alternatively, for a sweet version, leave out the olive oil and spread the bread with butter and honey before baking, and leave in the oven for 10 minutes. No extra topping is required.

Super Smoothie: Bananarama

For a smoothie that is really saying something . . . you will need:

1 very ripe banana
2 tsp honey or caster sugar
200 ml (6.75 fl oz) cold milk
1 scoop ice cream
a blender or liquidizer

1. Put the whole banana in the blender or let your child chop it carefully with a normal table knife before dropping it into the liquidizer, as he or she will enjoy being included in the chopping process.

2. Add the sugar or honey to the banana and blend to a puree. Then add the milk and ice cream and blend again.

3. Pour into a long glass and serve.

On special occasions you might want to add another scoop of ice cream on top and/or a sprinkle of grated chocolate. Yummy!

You can use the same method with any canned fruit and most berries. Strawberries and raspberries taste particularly good in smoothies.

A mother is a person who, seeing there are only four pieces of pie for five people, promptly announces she never did care for pie.
Tenneva Jordan

Salad Days

Children will always be able to help you to prepare a salad, even if they can't use a sharp knife. Let them wash the lettuce, and, if you have a lettuce dryer (one of those plastic, whirly drum things), they will thoroughly enjoy drying it too. Let them chop up things that aren't too tough, like hard-boiled eggs, but steer clear of giving them a sharp knife to tackle the carrots!

To make it more fun, try cutting silly shapes out of carrots, cucumber, etc. But don't try cutting tomatoes in half with a bevelled-edge knife. Life's too short!

Lassi Come Home

For a healthier drink, blend equal quantities of plain yogurt and milk with some honey. Add fruit if you wish. This drink is called Lassi and is served with many meals in India. It is particularly good if your child has a mild tummy upset.

Easy Peasy, Nice and Cheesy

This is incredibly easy and surprisingly delicious – and it might even encourage the kids to eat some vegetables.

You will need:
⅛ cup milk
½ cup cottage cheese
⅓ cup cream cheese
⅛ cup shredded mild Cheddar cheese
¼ cup soft cooked peas
⅛ cup diced cooked carrots
grated Parmesan cheese
shredded mozzarella cheese
a blender or liquidizer

1. Mix the milk, the cottage cheese, cream cheese and Cheddar cheese together in a blender or liquidizer until smooth, then stir in the peas and carrots.

2. Sprinkle with Parmesan cheese and shredded mozzarella cheese.

The finished product can be eaten on its own or as a side dish.

TIME FOR SOMETHING A LITTLE BIT HARDER

When your child has mastered the basics, and you have mastered the art of not pulling your hair out when it all goes wrong, you could try some of the following. But don't worry, it's not rocket science!

Piece of Fairy Cake

For those of us who didn't grow up around a cake-baking, jam-making kitchen queen, the word 'baking' can strike fear into our very core. Therefore, you should never feel you are underachieving in the parental stakes if you opt to buy a cake mix.

Children love to make cakes, and, for the younger ones, the mixing bowl provides most of the fun. The instructions are simple enough for all ages and the results are delicious. If you have visitors to share your creation with, you can always lie and say it was all your own work!

However, if you want to start from scratch, the easiest recipe is for fairy cakes. To make a dozen fairy cakes you will need:

For the cake mixture:
125 g (4.5 oz) softened butter
125 g (4.5 oz) caster sugar
2 eggs
125 g (4.5 oz) self-raising flour
2 tbsp milk
12 paper cases

For the icing:
115 g (4 oz) icing sugar
1–2 tbsp warm water

1 Beat the butter and sugar together until fluffy and light. Add one egg and stir in until the mixture is creamy and smooth, then add the second egg and do the same.

2 Sieve the flour into the mixture, then add the milk, and beat together.

3 Put the twelve cases on a baking tray and then divide the mixture into them using a spoon.

4 Bake in the oven for 15–20 minutes at 180°C (350°F or Gas mark 4), and then leave to cool on a wire rack.

5 For the icing, mix the icing sugar with 1–2 tbsp of warm water and spread over the cooled-down cakes. Ready-to-roll icing is also great fun and can easily be made into animal shapes or faces.

Let the kids decorate them as they wish. They can use dolly mixtures, hundreds and thousands, or Smarties. Or they can make funny faces using chocolate buttons and cake decorations.

Danish Delight

As a kid I loved making Danish Biscuit Cake (*Kiksekage*) with my mum, and I loved eating it even more! It's lovely as a treat with a cup of tea, but it is also a great dinner party pudding, served with ice cream. And it's really easy to make.

Though it used to be made with lard and raw eggs, it works just as well with the ingredients listed below.

300 g (10.5 oz) dark chocolate
350 ml (12 fl oz) whipping cream
100 g (3.5 oz) icing sugar
50 g (1.75 oz) unsalted butter
225 g (8 oz) plain biscuits
(morning coffee biscuits are the ideal shape,
but rich tea fingers work well too)

1 Chop the chocolate finely and put in a bowl.

2 Mix the whipping cream and icing sugar in a pan and bring carefully to the boil while stirring constantly. Pour the hot cream mix over the chocolate and stir from the middle of the bowl and out, until the chocolate has completely melted.

3 Break the butter into small pieces and stir into the chocolate mix. Place the bowl in the fridge for 15 minutes.

4 Cover a loaf tin, or a long, thin, rectangular container, with greaseproof paper. (To give you an idea of shape and size, we always used the plastic storage container designed for keeping packets of bacon.)

5 Spread a layer of the chocolate mix in the base of the tin. Cover with a layer of biscuits, then the chocolate mix, and so on, finishing with a layer of chocolate.

6 Cover the container with cling film and put in the fridge until the next day. When serving the cake, cut it carefully with a sharp, warmed knife. Be warned: it is very rich, so small pieces are advisable!

Something Fishy

Tuna and sweetcorn is a favourite with most kids, and these fishcakes are a tasty alternative to the standard fare of frozen fish fingers. To make eight fishcakes you will need the following:

> 500 g (1 lb) of potatoes, peeled and boiled
> 50 g (1.75 oz) butter
> 1 egg yolk
> 75 g (2.5 oz) plain flour
> 200 g (7 oz) can of tuna
> 200 g (7 oz) sweetcorn
> 150 g (5.5 oz) breadcrumbs
> 1 egg, beaten
> oil for frying

1 Mash the potatoes with the butter (the children love that bit), and stir in the egg yolk and the flour. Then add the tuna and sweetcorn, and some seasoning if desired, and stir well.

2 On a wooden board or plate, make eight oval shapes with the mixture and then pinch a tail shape in the end, to make a fish. Chill in the fridge for half an hour or so.

3 Dip the shapes into the beaten egg, then cover in breadcrumbs and fry for 3–4 minutes, until golden.

Serve with a healthy salad or some oven chips depending on your children's preference.

Flapjack Fun

These sweet treats are delicious – a firm favourite with most kids. They also contain both fruit and oats, so they're not too unhealthy either.

50 g (1.75 oz) sugar
50 g (1.75 oz) butter
(margarine can be used if preferred)
2 × 15 ml (0.5 fl oz) spoons golden syrup
150 g (5.5 oz) oats
75 g (2.5 oz) dried fruit, (e.g. sliced apricots,
raisins, sultanas, mixed fruit)
a shallow baking tin

1 Grease a shallow baking tin and line with greaseproof paper (the kids can do the messy bit, while you can measure and cut out the right amount of paper).

2 Place the sugar, butter and syrup into a saucepan and gently heat until the butter has melted. Then stir in the oats.

3 Pour half of the mixture into the baking tin and arrange the dried fruit over the oaty mixture. Then pour the remaining mixture over the fruit and pat down.

4 Bake for 20 minutes at 200°C (400°F or Gas mark 6) or until lightly browned.

5 Remove from the oven and cut into portions in the baking tin while hot. Use an oven glove or tea towel to hold the tin steady. Try not to burn yourself – and don't let a young child help with that bit!

Supercool Sarnies

Kids love making their own sandwiches, but you may find that they get bored with traditional ingredients. Try combining a few different things to make their sarnies more interesting.

✳ Tuna and egg mayonnaise

✳ Egg and sweetcorn mayonnaise

✳ Peanut butter and cucumber

✳ Avocado and chicken

✳ Mozzarella and tomato
(this is even better if lightly toasted)

✳ Ham and cheese

✳ Bacon, lettuce and tomato (BLT)

Also, try some different breads such as focaccia, ciabatta and pitta.

Sailboat Sandwiches

These snacks are such fun to make, because they look like yachts and taste great. You will need:

> *oval-shaped rolls, such as sub rolls*
> *peanut butter, tuna mayonnaise, cream cheese*
> *or other 'sticky' ingredients*
> *1 banana (if using peanut butter)*
> *or sweetcorn (if using tuna)*
> *sliced cheddar cheese*

1. Slice the roll in half to make two boat shapes, and spread the sticky ingredients on to the exposed part of the roll to cover the middle section of the 'boat'.

2. Use another ingredient, such as banana or sweetcorn, to create a rim around the edge of the 'deck'. If you prefer, use three different ingredients to make it more colourful. You could add ham slivers around the edge or cucumber funnels.

3. Finally, make a sail for the sailing ship by putting a cocktail stick through some sliced cheddar cheese, or ham, and stand it in the middle of the boat.

These sarnies are great for parties or just for a fun lunch.

A Mother's Wisdom

(Or, things your mother told you . . .
and the scientific truth)

'If you swallow chewing gum it will stay in your digestive system for seven years.'

The Truth: Chewing gum, like anything else, stays in your digestive system for an average of about twenty hours as roughage.

*

'If you don't wait an hour after eating to go swimming, you will get a cramp and die.'

The Truth: No death has ever been attributed to entering a pool too quickly after eating, although a huge meal, followed by excessive exercise, could cause cramp or indigestion.

*

'One hundred strokes with a brush is good for your hair.'

The Truth: This myth came about when people rarely washed their hair, but now that we wash our hair more frequently, the opposite is true. Excessive brushing wears away the hair's cuticle making it more matted and tangly, and causing split ends.

**'Your hair will grow back thicker and darker
after you've shaved it.'**

The Truth: Hair may seem to grow back thicker
because short hairs tend to feel and look dark and coarse,
but it's an illusion.

*

**'If you pull ugly faces your face will stay that way
if the wind changes.'**

The Truth: Clearly, there is no scientific basis for this old
wives' tale – although some of the faces you see on a windy
day are worth worrying about!

'Sweets will rot your teeth.'

The Truth: Obviously there's some truth in this (and we
wouldn't advise telling your children it's not true!), but some
carbohydrates such as pasta and soft breads can do more
damage than sugar because acid is formed by the food
remnants in the mouth. Saliva can fully dissolve sugar,
but not these 'fermentable carbohydrates'.

'Eat up your carrots – they're good for your eyes.'

The Truth: The beta-carotene in carrots is an excellent source of vitamin A, and a deficiency of this vitamin causes night blindness. But in developed countries, vitamin A deficiency is virtually non-existent.

∗

'If you eat up your crusts they'll make your hair curl.'

The Truth: Although crusts are good for you, as the browning reaction on the surface of the bread produces antioxidants, there is no evidence to suggest that eating them has any effect on your hairstyle!

∗

'If you go out with wet hair you'll catch a cold.'

The Truth: You may well feel colder if you go outside with wet hair, but that won't make you any more susceptible to colds. Viruses cause colds and getting cold doesn't.

∗

'Chicken soup is good for colds.'

The Truth: This is actually true because chicken soup is thought to boost the immune system by stopping the movement of white blood cells that stimulate the release of mucus. It's also packed with nutrition, is easy to swallow and will help to keep you hydrated. Not to mention that it's tasty comfort food (as long as you're not a vegetarian!).

'Stop cracking your knuckles – you'll get arthritis.'

The Truth: This is a myth, although knuckle-cracking can lead to cartilage damage.

✳

'If you're pregnant and your "bump" is all in the front, you'll have a boy.'

The Truth: The shape of your bump has more to do with the position of the baby than its sex. If its back is facing away from Mum's spine, it's more likely to stick out at the front.

'An apple a day keeps the doctor away.'

The Truth: Any fresh fruit, eaten on a regular basis, help to keep you healthy. Apples, in particular, are good sources of flavonoids, which might have anti-carcinogenic effects.

✳

'Feed a cold, starve a fever.'

The Truth: If you have a fever, your metabolic rate increases and burns energy more quickly. This means it's best not to starve and it's vital to drink lots of fluids. Feeding a cold will have no beneficial effect unless it is with food rich in vitamin C.

Mum's the Word

Anecdotes and stories on mothers

Minnie, the mother of the Marx Brothers, had a sense of humour to match that of her sons. 'Because we were a kid act, we travelled at half-fare, despite the fact that we were all around twenty,' Groucho once recalled. 'Minnie insisted we were thirteen . . .'

"That kid of yours is in the dining car smoking a cigar," the conductor told her. "And another one is in the washroom shaving." Minnie shook her head sadly and said, "They grow so fast!"'

One morning while attending Timbertops School in Australia, Prince Charles attended a service at the local parish church. The rector spoke to the Prince after the service and apologized for the small turnout.

'Being bank holiday weekend,' he explained, 'most of the parishioners are away.'

'Not another bank holiday!' the prince exclaimed. 'What's this one in aid of?'

'Well,' the rector replied, rather embarrassed, 'over here we call it the Queen's birthday.'

Charlie Chaplin grew up in poverty in South London. When he rose to fame he adopted his famous Tramp costume as a trademark. The first time his mother saw him wearing it she exclaimed, 'Charlie, I have to get you a new suit!'

✳

Johnny Depp likes to remember events in his life with a tattoo. Among the etchings on his body he has the legend Wino Forever, which used to say Winona Forever, but was altered when he split with former fiancée Winona Ryder. He also has a Cherokee Indian chief on his right arm and his mother's name, Betty Sue, tattooed on his left.

✳

Playing the title role in *Oliver Twist* (1922), Jackie Coogan was required to cry on cue. When asked 'Where's your muvver?' he was to reply, 'My mother is dead, sir,' and burst into tears. However, the eight-year-old actor couldn't force himself to cry. Frank Lloyd, the film's director, suggested that he try to imagine that his mother really was dead, but still the tears refused to come. Suddenly, the young Jackie had an idea. 'Mr Lloyd,' he said, 'would it be all right if I imagine that my dog is dead?'

✳

At the tender age of six, Shirley Temple stopped believing in Santa Claus. 'Mother took me to see him in a department store,' she later explained. 'He asked for my autograph, and said he saw all my movies.'

'Me Time' For Mums: Perfect Pampering

When you've spent all day running around after your demanding brood, it's time to treat yourself like a princess and enjoy a bit of self-pampering. Trying to fit everything into your busy schedule is exhausting and, let's face it, being the perfect mum you are, your need for a good time is usually last on the list of priorities. But 'me time' is a must if you're going to preserve your sanity and maintain your role as Supermum.

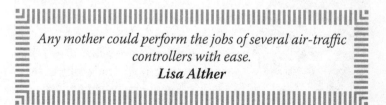

Any mother could perform the jobs of several air-traffic controllers with ease.
Lisa Alther

PAMPER PARTIES

Trying to fit in a social life, a manicure and some much-needed relaxation is very difficult, but this activity kills these three birds with one stone. There are various companies that provide this service and you can get information about them by asking in your local beauty shop or surfing the net.

When you've found a pampering service that suits your needs, call a group of friends and invite them to your house (making sure that all male partners are out of the way for the duration!), then prepare the living room with scented candles and nibbles, and open a bottle of wine. The beauty therapist will do the rest. You can get treatments from massages to manicures, pedicures and facials, as well as having a good gossip with your mates. If all goes well, you'll find yourself in an unbelievably relaxed state of mind by the end of the evening.

GET A NEW HAIRDO

Looking better inevitably makes you feel better, so if you haven't changed your hairstyle for a while, book an appointment with a good hairdresser and go for it. It might only take an hour, but it makes all the difference.

SOAK IT ALL AWAY

Though it's a cliché, a long, hot bath can relax you in a way that no other activity can. The ancient Greek and Romans used hydrotherapy to cure stress, aches and anxiety, and it is still used in medicine today. Light some scented candles and add some

aromatherapy oil or bubble bath to the water, and take in a book or magazine – then soak up the benefits.

In *The Bathtub Yoga & Relaxation Book*, author Margaret Jaffe says, 'You forget how to take care of yourself, and [a bath] teaches you to take time, meditate and be mindful of your body.' It also has the added benefit of you being in a room with a locked door!

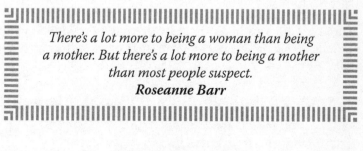

There's a lot more to being a woman than being a mother. But there's a lot more to being a mother than most people suspect.
Roseanne Barr

THE DATING GAME

She may be a working mother with two young children, but Michelle Pfeiffer still 'dates' her husband, David E. Kelly. 'David

and I have date nights when we go out to the movies,' she says. 'It's one of my favourite things to do and it helps keep the marriage alive.' But if you can't get a babysitter, why not bring the cinema to your home? Buy some popcorn, dim the lights and hire a DVD – then snuggle up to your partner with a glass of wine.

If movies aren't your thing, recreate a favourite holiday destination in your own home. If you love Italy, for example, cook a special pasta meal, lay a checked tablecloth with scented candles, and reminisce about a romantic holiday that you both shared. If you don't have a partner, do something similar with the kids. It will make a refreshing change to an ordinary family meal.

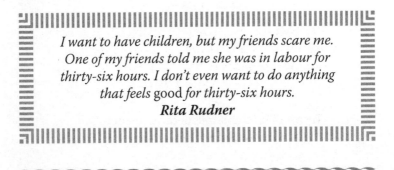

I want to have children, but my friends scare me. One of my friends told me she was in labour for thirty-six hours. I don't even want to do anything that feels good for thirty-six hours.
Rita Rudner

Things My Mother Taught Me

My mother taught me about patience...
'Just wait until your father gets home.'

❋

My mother taught me about receiving...
'You are really going to get it when we get home!'

❋

My mother taught me to meet a challenge...
*'What were you thinking? Answer me when I talk to you!
Don't talk back to me!'*

❋

My mother taught me logic...
*'If you fall out off that swing and break your neck,
you're not going to the shops with me.'*

❋

My mother taught me medical science...
'If you sit too close to the TV, your eyes will go square.'

My mother taught me to think long term . . .
***'If you don't pass your spelling test,
you'll never get a good job.'***

∗

My mother taught me ESP . . .
***'Put your sweater on; don't you think I know when
you're cold?'***

∗

My mother taught me humour . . .
'When you break a leg, don't come running to me.'

∗

My mother taught me about genetics . . .
'You're just like your father.'

∗

My mother taught me about my roots . . .
'You weren't born in a barn, you know!'

∗

My mother taught me about the wisdom of age . . .
'When you get to be my age, you will understand.'

∗

My mother taught me about justice . . .
***'One day you'll have kids, and I hope they turn out
just like you . . . Then you'll see what it's like.'***

Halloween Queen

Everybody loves Halloween and entering into the spirit of the occasion doesn't have to take much time or money. To throw the best Halloween party in town, all you need are a few shortcuts and a spooky sense of humour!

FRIGHTENING FOOD

Use a cutter to make ghost-shaped sandwiches or witches hats. If you don't have the correctly shaped cutter, draw a picture of a ghost or witch's hat, and cut round the shape with a sharp knife.

*

Scoop out the insides of a pumpkin and fill it with bug- and snake-shaped sweets. It looks really effective if they're spilling out over the side.

Slice off the top of an orange, scoop out the insides and cut a pumpkin face into one side. Then fill the orange with ice cream, and put the top back on. Each icy orange can be kept in the freezer until it's time to eat them.

Spider Cakes

Cover some fairy cakes (see page 76 for the recipe) with chocolate icing and add chocolate sticks (perhaps Matchmakers) for legs. Jelly tots make great eyes too, and you can decorate the cakes with other sweets if you wish to make your spider more colourful.

Eggy Eyeballs

1 Make some hard-boiled eggs and wait for them to cool.

2 Slice each of them in half, width wise, scoop out the yolk and fill the holes with cream cheese.

3 Add a pimento-stuffed olive, which has been sliced in half with the pimento showing.

4 Then dip a cocktail stick in red food dye and draw veiny lines across the white of the eggs to make them look really bloodshot.

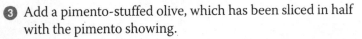

Evil Eggs

These eggs look really effective, but you'll have to prepare them the day before.

1. Cook some hard-boiled eggs and cool them in cold water.

2. Crack the shells all over with the back of a spoon, taking care not to break pieces off.

3. Place the eggs in a bowl of cold water with a tablespoon of food colouring (whichever colour you prefer) and leave them for eight hours or overnight.

4. Remove the shells and place the discoloured eggs in a 'nest' of grated carrot and shredded lettuce.

Creepy-crawly Jelly

1. Buy some chewy creepy-crawly or snake sweets and place some in the bottom of a glass bowl. Then make up half a packet of jelly and pour the liquid on top.

2. When the jelly has set, add some more creepy crawlies and cover with the remaining jelly mixture.

A word of warning – don't leave the jelly for too long after making it, as the sweets tend to swell up!

Being a mother is a profession just like being a doctor or a lawyer, except that if you have several children it's more like being an Indian chief.
Author unknown

Hot Frogs

1. Roll out some ready-made puff pastry and use a frog-shaped cutter, or make a frog-shaped template to cut round, and create some frog shapes measuring approximately 13×12.75 cm (5.5 × 5 inches). Place them on a baking sheet and gently prick their tummies with a fork.

2. Take some green apples and cut them in half, cutting out the core and pips. Fill the hollow with mince-meat or raisins soaked in orange juice.

3. Brush the pastry frogs with some milk or soft butter, and place half an apple on each frog's tummy, skin side up.

4. Use raisins for their eyes, then place the pastry frogs in the oven and bake for 15–20 minutes at 200°C (400°F or Gas mark 6), until golden.

5. Serve with coloured custard or green ice cream.

EASY-TO-MAKE HALLOWEEN COSTUMES

Bats

To form the basis of the costume, all you need is a black leotard or a tight-fitting black T-shirt and tights, and you can easily make some bat wings yourself.

1 Take a large piece of black material (felt is best as it doesn't fray) and cut out two large bat-wing shapes, making sure that the length of the wing measures the same as the distance from your child's wrist to the top of his/her shoulder.

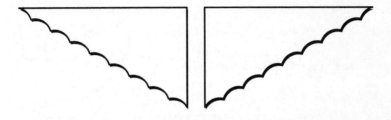

2 Sew a loop of black elastic to the underside end of each wing (wide enough to fit your child's wrists through), and then sew or pin the other end of the bat wings to the back of the leotard or T-shirt.

3 To make a simple hood, measure your child's head from the forehead over the top of the head to the back of the neck, then measure the distance from one ear to the middle of the back of the head and from one ear to midway under the chin. Take a piece of black furry fabric or black felt and use the measurements when drawing two hood and two bat-ear shapes on the material (see examples overleaf), and then cut them out.

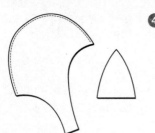

④ Sew the two hood shapes together with the fur sides touching, then turn inside out. Next, sew the ears in place on the top of the hood, and add a strip of Velcro at the chin to ensure that the hood stays on more easily.

⑤ If you find that your bat ears are a bit too floppy, try cutting out four larger ear shapes and sewing two of each together, leaving a gap at the bottom that is wide enough to fit an ear-shaped piece of card. The card should make the bat ears more rigid before they are properly attached to the hood.

Trash Trolls

This is a simple, effective costume that doesn't require any sewing, which is always a good thing!

① Take a black tie-top binliner and cut arm holes just below the ties. Then cut off the base of the sack making a zigzag effect on the bottom. Lengthwise it should hang above your child's feet.

② Using spray paint and leaf stencils (the latter either shop-bought or cut from stiff cardboard with a craft knife), spray overlapping leaf designs in bright, autumnal colours on to the binliner.

③ When the paint has dried, put the costume on a willing child, drawing the strings loosely round his/her neck and tying the ties into a bow.

④ Add tights or leggings, then mess up their hair and colour with spray-on (non-permanent) dye and firm-hold hairspray to make it look nice and wild. Brown face paint can also be added, to look like smeared dirt. It's probably the only time you'll let your kids get away with looking so messy, so let them savour the moment!

Please note: this is not a recommended costume for very young children due to the risk of suffocation or choking.

Wicked Queen

① Fold a large piece of purple or red felt in half and cut out a basic cape shape (see page 26).

② Cut vertical slits below the neckline and run enough ribbon through to tie into a bow around the neck (see page 27).

③ Add three 6.5 cm- (2.5 inch-) wide strips of fake fur across the top and down the sides of the cape using glue or stitching.

④ Dress your child in a black outfit, such as black top, skirt and tights.

⑤ For a wicked crown, cut a piece of black card into the shape of a crown and glue on some colourful plastic gems.

⑥ Add costume jewellery and finish with wicked joke nails, spooky make-up and a wand.

Count Dracula

1. Create a cape out of black felt.

2. Slick back hair and add joke fangs.

3. Use white face make-up to make the skin look pale and a black eyebrow pencil to create some arched brows and a pointed hairline, then add a dab of red lipstick to the lips.

Scary Mummy

1. Wrap your little one in bandages (or ripped up strips of old white sheets) leaving his or her face bandage-free.

2. For the finishing touch, cover their face with white make-up.

The Hunchback of Notre Dame

1. Create the 'hunchback' effect by packing foam or cardboard inside a cloth bag or an old pair of tights.

2. Pin the hump to an old baggy T-shirt or shirt, and find an old coat several sizes too large to wear over the humpbacked shirt.

3. Add some baggy pyjama trousers and a straggly wig.

HALLOWEEN GAMES

Apple Bobbing

Firstly, tie a long piece of string, horizontally, from two fixed objects (perhaps a banister or a coat rack), above head height. Then, using some apples with sturdy stalks, tie smaller lengths of string to each apple stalk and fasten the other end to the horizontal string, in a row, making sure that each apple dangles close enough to the children's heads. The kids must try to bite the apples without using their hands. If you'd prefer to do this outdoors, you could make use of an empty washing line, and simply tie the apples on a string to the line overhead.

Wrap the Mummy

Divide the kids into two teams and choose a 'mummy'. Then provide each team with a roll of toilet paper and tell them to 'wrap the mummy'. The first team to wrap their mummy, leaving just the eyes and nose showing, is the winner.

Murder in the Dark
(for children of eight years or over)

Depending on how many children are playing the game, you need to prepare beforehand by writing on several pieces of paper each of the roles that the children will have to play.

Firstly, write the word 'Murderer' on one, 'Detective' on another, and on each of the remaining pieces of paper write the word 'Suspect'. Fold up each bit of paper to the same size, place them in a bag and let each child pick one, making sure that they keep the contents a secret from everyone else. Next, turn off the lights. (Do make sure that any furniture with sharp edges has been moved out of the way to avoid accidents!)

To kill anyone the murderer simply has to tap them on the shoulder. When this happens the suspects must let out an anguished cry and fall down 'dead'. The murderer can have more than one victim, and the lights go back on after a minute or two. However, if the detective is killed, he/she must call out 'Detective is dead', and the lights go on immediately. Everyone stays where they are: the victims on the floor and the suspects (and the murderer) still standing. It's up to the detective to discover the identity of the murderer by asking questions such as 'Did you see anything suspicious?' and by observing the body language and facial expressions of each of the suspects for signs of guilt e.g. giggling!

The detective has five minutes to work out who the murderer is. If he/she guesses correctly, the detective is the winner, but if he/she is wrong, the murderer wins the game.

Touchy-feely Scary Story

You will need:
a large cardboard box
a pumpkin
a feather
a small furry toy
some twigs
some jelly
tinned lychees or fresh peeled grapes
cold spaghetti

Cut a hole in the front and back of a large cardboard box, so that you can place each item inside from the back as and when it is mentioned in the story, keeping it hidden under a cloth so that it can't be seen as it is moved.

Turn the lights down low and tell a scary story, getting the children to put their hands into the front of the box and feel each item as it occurs in the tale. You can make up your own story or use this one. You can also use your own children's names if you like.

In a deep, dark cave, in a deep, dark wood, lived a wicked, old witch.

One night, as a full moon rose in the sky, Georgia and Joe were walking through the deep, dark wood on their way home. Playing together happily, Joe ran into the trees and his sister chased him, deeper and deeper until, suddenly, they realized they were lost.

Suddenly feeling frightened, Joe began to cry, but his big sister put on her bravest face. 'We'll be fine, Joe,' she said. 'Let's find somewhere to shelter until the morning,

when it's light, and we'll soon be able to find our way home.'

At that moment Georgia spotted a cave. 'In here, Joe,' she said. 'This will do.'

But as they entered the cave, the children could hear an eerie whisper. They reached out their hands and touched the slimy wall (**the lid of the pumpkin**). Then, slowly, they moved inside the cave and Joe put his hand on a rock. Wriggling worms squelched between his fingers (**cooked spaghetti**). Joe backed away just as something crawled across Georgia's hand (**feather**).

The children were really frightened, but something was calling them into the cave. The whispers were getting louder and they couldn't seem to run away. Suddenly they felt something furry brush against them (**furry toy**) and they screamed. A cat ran away into the cave, and, as soon as it had gone, a faint light could be seen at the end of a dark tunnel.

'Let's see what it is,' said Georgia, who was too curious to be afraid now. Teeth chattering, Joe followed her down the corridor. As they neared the light, though, it grew dim and a cackle was heard in the gloom.

'Come in children,' said an old woman's voice. 'I won't bite.' A loud cackle split the air again.

Georgia and Joe reached out and touched the woman's bony finger (**a twig**).

'It's all right, children,' she cackled again. 'Come in and have something to eat.'

Joe, who loved his food, moved forward into a round chamber where a little fire glowed. On the fire sat a cauldron, and, sitting beside it glaring, was a black cat.

The old lady offered the children three dishes but it was too dark to see what was inside so they put their fingers in to feel.

First they felt something hard (**small twigs**). 'What's this?' they asked.

'Bats' claws,' answered the witch, quietly.

Then they felt something squishy (**jelly**). 'What's that?' they asked.

'Toads' intestines,' answered the witch, quietly.

Next they felt something round and squashy (**lychees or peeled grapes**). 'What's this?' they asked.

'CHILDREN'S EYEBALLS!' shouted the witch.

The children screamed and then ran and ran until they reached the other side of the woods where they found their mum and dad, who had been very worried about them and were out looking for them. And, funnily enough, Georgia and Joe never went into the woods again!

THE END

Record-Breaking Mums

Anything we can do, they can do better! If you think you've had a big baby, or more children than you can shake a stick at, take a look at this impressive bunch.

The record for the most children born to one woman is a staggering sixty-nine. The wife of an eighteenth-century Russian peasant was reported to have been pregnant twenty-seven times and had sixteen sets of twins, seven sets of triplets and four sets of quadruplets. That's a hell of a lot of washing . . .

✳

The heaviest baby ever born was to Canadian Anna Bates in 1879. Her baby boy weighed 23 lb 12 oz (10.8 kg). Ouch!

✳

In the UK, the heaviest baby recorded was reported in a letter from a doctor to the *British Medical Journal* in 1879. It claimed that a child born in 1852, in Cornwall, weighed 21 lb (9.5 kg). When did this huge bundle arrive? On Christmas Day, of course.

American mothers Laura Shelley and Caroline Cargado share a record achievement. Both women have had two sets of twins who share the same birthday. Laura gave birth to Melissa Nicole and Mark Fredrick Julian Jr in 1990, followed by Kayla May and Jonathan Price Moore in 2003, all on 25 March. Caroline had Keilani Marie and Kahleah Mae in 1996, then Mikayla Anee and Malia Abigail in 2003 on 30 May.

✳

Lisa Coffey, from Virginia, USA, is the proud mother of the lightest surviving triplets ever. Born by emergency Caesarean on 30 November 1998, they had a combined weight of 3 lb 0.8 oz (1.38 kg). Peyton weighed in at 1 lb 3.6 oz (583 g), Jackson 13.8 oz (320 g) and Blake 13.3 oz (380 g). The babies spent nearly four months in hospital before they were allowed home, but they are now fit, healthy kids – and no doubt quite a handful.

✳

Maddalena Granata, from Nocera in Italy, was born in 1839, married at twenty-eight and gave birth to fifteen sets of triplets. In total she had fifty-two children, forty-nine of whom were boys.

Mary Jonas of the UK (who died in 1899) gave birth to fifteen sets of twins, all of which were of a boy-girl combination.

*

The oldest woman to have become a mother is Adriana Iliescu of Romania. After undergoing fertility treatment, she gave birth to a baby girl in January 2005, at the age of sixty-six. 'Each person has a mission in life, and maybe this was my mission,' said the happy mum on the birth of Eliza Maria. Dr Bogdan Marinescu, who carried out the fertility treatment, earlier justified the procedure by saying Adriana was in an appropriate condition to give birth. But the birth of Eliza led to calls by Romanian officials for a public debate on the medical and ethical consequences of fertility treatments.

*

Dr Patricia Rashbrook caused controversy when she became the oldest woman in the UK to give birth at the age of sixty-two. Dr Rashbrook, who had three grown-up children from a previous marriage, travelled to Eastern Europe to receive fertility treatment from Italian expert Severino Antinori, and in May 2006 gave birth to a healthy 6lb 10.5oz (3.02kg) boy, nicknamed JJ. She dismissed her critics and declared: 'He is adorable, and seeing him for the first time was beyond words. Having been through so much to have him, we are overjoyed. His birth is absolutely wonderful.' Should the age of his mother cause JJ any anxiety when he gets older, at least she will be qualified to deal with it. Dr Rashbrook is a child psychiatrist.

On 25 July 1978, Lesley Brown gave birth to a 5 lb 12 oz (2.61 kg) daughter and made history. The baby was Louise Joy Brown, the world's first IVF baby. Lesley and husband John had been trying to conceive for nine years, but in 1977 help appeared in the pioneering form of Patrick Steptoe and Robert Edwards, who had been working on the concept of 'in vitro fertilization'. The Browns consented to the experiment and Louise was the happy result. Since Louise's birth, millions of babies have been born through IVF. Happily she is now a mum herself, having conceived naturally.

You're Not Going Out Dressed Like That!

Mums have a duty to look their best when they go out in public with their children. To spare your children's embarrassment you should never go for the 'mutton dressed as lamb' look or turn up at the school gates in your pyjamas.

Getting the look right doesn't mean you have to look 'mumsy', but there a few fashion faux pas that should be avoided by any mum over the age of twenty-five.

✳

Midriff tops – few women have the stomach for it, literally!

✳

Miniskirts – there comes a time when, no matter how fashionable minis or how shapely your legs are, the hemline should start to drop.

✳

Tight, slogan-covered T-shirts – even if the slogan is hilariously funny, it won't be for long. If the slogan is rude, you will cause maximum embarrassment to your children; if the slogan is 'Babe' or any other reference to the physical beauty of the wearer, you had better be able to live up to it!

Leggings – Lycra leggings have made something of a comeback, but they *must* be worn with a long top, otherwise, don't ask 'does my bum look big in this?' because it definitely will!

✳

Hotpants – even worse than minis, for all sorts of reasons . . . cellulite being the most obvious!

✳

Tracksuit bottoms – they are fine for the gym, but they should be confined to sit-ups and press-ups, not school pick-ups.

✳

Twinset and pearls – unless you have a title and are picking the children up from Eton, it's best to avoid the upper-class frump look.

✳

Thigh-length boots – domestic and dominatrix are rarely found in the same sentence.

✳

A baseball cap – worn on anyone over the age of twenty, these can cause major embarrassment, especially if you wear them back to front!

✳

A pink Mohican – enough said.

Oh, Mum!

(Or, things you should never do when you're a mum)

Make your children's clothes

✳

Wear your children's clothes

✳

Make your child wear hand-me-downs that are too big,
too small or contain holes

✳

Make a girl wear big brother's hand-me-downs

✳

Make a boy wear pink

✳

Say 'I told you so' when your child falls off the chair
he's been standing on and cracks his head open

Cut your child's hair

✻

Make your children kiss terrifying old relatives

✻

Date your son's friends

✻

Show nude baby photos of your teenage son
to his mates or girlfriend

Rainy Day Play

Having just promised the kids they can go to the park, you pull back the curtains and see sheets of rain falling from the skies. You'll need to think quickly to stem the flow of wailing and protesting from your little gems, who just don't seem to understand why rain should stop play.

But all is not lost. All you need is a little imagination and a lot of patience, and a wet afternoon can be a joy for ever.

Junk Modelling

This needs some forward planning, as saving cereal boxes, washing-up liquid containers and the inside tube of kitchen rolls is required. Other useful packages include Pringle tubes, egg boxes, yogurt cartons and Smartie tubes.

Grab as many empty containers as you can lay your hands on and put them in a pile in the middle of a table. Spread out sheets of newspaper across the table, so the kids can make as much mess as they want without ruining the surface beneath, and provide them with child-safe glue, scissors and sticky tape. Your preparation work done, then you can safely leave them to it. The only drawback is that once your children have presented you with the car/rocket/bus that they have lovingly made, you will be forced to treat it as a Rodin sculpture, put it on display, and promise *never* to throw it away. Of course, if you allow a respectable amount of time to pass you can hide it and, eventually, when they've forgotten about it, consign it to the dustbin (only joking!).

Home Cinema

Rather than sticking them in front of the telly, make a cinema experience in your own front room. Rent a new video or DVD, or find an old one you haven't seen for a while, then draw all the curtains and turn the lights out.

Popcorn, ice cream or ice lollies will make it feel more like a cinema, and, if you have a popcorn maker or a microwave, making the popcorn can be part of the fun. If your children don't like popcorn, cut up pieces of fruit and put them in a popcorn bucket or large drinking cup.

OK, so they're still sitting in front of the telly, but at least you've put some thought into it!

Chart Hit

Ask your children to make a chart about themselves. Each chart should contain the name and age of the child and some personal details, such as height, hair colour and eye colour. Then they can add a list of their favourite things, including favourite colour, animal TV programme and pop song.

They'll have loads of fun making the charts, and, if they make them at regular intervals, they will be a novel way of seeing how your child changes as he or she grows up. Keep them all together and, when they are older, you can spend another rainy afternoon going through them together.

Designer T-shirt

Kids love to decorate clothing and they will enjoy wearing the result. Give each child a light-coloured, plain T-shirt and a packet of fabric crayons or paints, which can be bought in most big supermarkets or in a craft shop. Insert a large piece of cardboard into the T-shirt, as this will stop it from bunching up.

For best results, make sure the kids work out their design on a piece of paper first, otherwise you'll end up with a designer dog's dinner which nobody in their right mind would wear.

Dressing-up Day

When you clear out the wardrobe you may want to chuck most of your clothes away or give them to the local charity shop, but keep a few choice items aside to use for dressing up.

Dresses and skirts are ideal, as are a few loose tops, old jewellery and the odd pair of trousers. If you can spare the space, put them in an old suitcase or a toybox and the kids have an instant game on any wet day.

If you add a few cheap wigs and old hats that you've picked up cheaply at a local charity shop, the comedy effect is well worth it!

Taste Test

Select eight different foods and put them in small bowls. Then label them with numbers 1–8. The best foods include yogurt, mousse, mashed banana, porridge, pasta or pizza sauce, salad dressings and lemon curd.

Allow each child to taste a tiny bit from each bowl and write down (or tell you, if they are too young to write) what they think each one is. This works better if you blindfold them or, if you prefer, add some colouring to disguise the food. The winner is the one who guesses the most correctly.

Treasure Hunt

Hide gifts or treats around the house for each child, and lay a trail of clues. Each clue should lead to another until the final hiding place is found, but make sure that you take each child's age into account.

To make it more fun (for you as well as them) try writing the clues in rhyme. For example:

> *By a mirror, near a door*
> *You will find clue number four*

Outdoor Fun with the Kids

The sun is shining, the weather is mild and *still* the kids would rather sit in front of the TV than go out and play in the garden. Theme parks and fun fairs are a great idea to get them out of the house, as long as you don't mind spending an absolute fortune to get in, before queuing for an hour on each ride. But if your idea of fun is ending up terrified out of your wits and soaked to the skin because the kids want one more go on the log ride, go ahead.

If your nerves and your finances are important to you, however, try some of the safer and cheaper suggestions below.

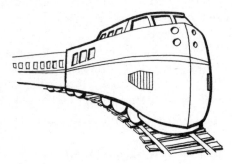

On the Buses

In the age of two-car families, it's surprising how exciting public transport can be for children. Get a bus or a train to your local town and look round the shops or just have a coffee. The journey is the thing and the kids will love it. Make sure you check the timetable first, though. They won't be quite so happy if they have to wait half an hour at the bus stop or on a blustery platform!

Let's Go Fly a Kite

An obvious and traditional family pastime, it's surprising how few people actually go out and do it. Kites are very cheap these days and then all you need is a windy heath or field. The beach is an ideal place, as winds tend to be stronger on the coast, but they're best avoided at the height of summer; bikini-clad sun worshippers tend not to take too kindly to a kite dropping on their well-oiled tummies!

A Walk in the Woods

As long as it's not tipping down, a long walk can be loads of fun with the whole family. If it is a little wet, get the kids wrapped up in macs and wellies.

To make it more fun, provide them with a list of things to look or listen out for in the woods and get them to cross off the items on the list as they go. They can look for easy items like twigs, bluebells and toadstools, as well as harder items like ladybirds, sparrows, conkers and specific trees or berries, or listening out for specific birdcalls. A word of warning though – don't encourage them to take too many things home with them, unless you want a house full of creepy crawlies!

You don't have to go it alone. Invite along some friends who also have children and you'll find the moans of 'Oh Mum, I hate walks!' soon die down.

Pick Your Own

Many a happy childhood hour has been whiled away picking strawberries, raspberries, and blackberries. If you are lucky, this might just mean strolling down a country lane with a basket or bucket, but if there are no wild berries nearby, try to find a farm in the area that has a Pick Your Own policy.

The kids have loads of fun and it even encourages them to eat the fruits of their labour, which is never a bad thing. The hardest part is getting them to put the fruit into the container before they put it into their mouths!

Party in the Park

Whether you live in a town or a village, there will nearly always be a park just around the corner – and that's all you need for a party. Invite some friends, ask everyone to bring along some picnic items, then you can make a day of it. Organize games of rounders, catch or just take a football. The kids will be happy, and you and your friends get to have a good natter.

Alternatively, if you have a big enough garden, why not make the most of some decent weather and the open space on your doorstep. Prepare some picnic food, take a blanket out into the garden and have your own little family party there.

Be a Tourist

We all seek out the local attractions while we are on holiday and usually end up armed with hundreds of leaflets with ideas of what to do. But how many of us every do it in our local town?

Whether it's London, Manchester, Glasgow or smaller towns throughout the country, many may have hidden gems you never knew were there. Even if you've lived there all your life, it's worth popping into the Tourist Information Centre and finding out what is going on. There will be child-friendly museums, art galleries and attractions which are cheap, if not free, and you'll have a great time exploring your own city.

Farm Them Out

Many areas, even in the inner cities, now have farms that welcome visitors, where kids can get close to the animals. For city farms in your area log on to www.farmgarden.org.uk or contact the Federation of City Farms and Community Gardens on 0117 923 1800.

A word of warning: Children love to pet farm animals, but it is not always hygienic. If they are allowed contact, the farm has to have washing stations so do make sure the children wash their hands properly after touching each animal.

Also, some farms have animals for sale. Be sure you can resist pester power – or you might find yourself with a cute little lamb in the back garden, which will quickly become a grown-up sheep!

Swim For It

Local swimming pools are usually quite cheap and kids love to play in the water. Take toys for the children to dive for, and a small floating ball to play catch with. If you don't fancy swimming, find out what else is on at the local leisure centre, as many have trampolining, soft play areas, and tennis and badminton courts.

Have a Ball on the Beach

If you don't fancy kite-flying, why not grab a bucket and take your kids on a hunt for different types of seashells. They are great to take home to decorate boxes, to stick on card to create interesting collages or just to give a finishing touch to a carefully constructed sandcastle. Buy a little sea-life guide and take your kids exploring in the rock pools and streams around the beach, identifying the plants and creatures living in them. (If you don't want to buy a book, have a look on the Internet and print off some relevant information.)

Alternatively, if there are three or more of you, bring along a cricket bat and a tennis ball and have a game of French Cricket (but watch out for those pesky sunbathers).

The Rules:

The first batsman should draw a circle around himself, using the cricket bat at arm's length. Then one fielder bowls (underarm) from a few yards in front of the batsman, who must hit it away without moving his feet. The next fielder bowls from wherever the ball falls, even if it is behind the batsman – and the batsman must *never* move his feet.

His legs are the wicket and he will be out if:

    (a) the ball hits his legs;
    (b) his feet move;
    (c) he falls and his hand touches the floor;
    (d) he fails to hit the ball out of the circle;
    (e) he hits the ball twice;
    (f) the ball is caught before hitting the ground.

If he is not out, he scores one run. The bowler gives the batsman a run if:

    (a) the ball bounces outside the circle before entering it;
    (b) the ball is not bowled between the batsman's feet and shoulders;
    (c) the ball is bowled overarm.

The fielder who gets the batsman out is the next to bat.

It's a great game and often ends up looking like you're playing Twister, especially when the batsman tries to hit a ball from behind without moving his legs or falling over!

Are We Nearly There Yet?

Children love going on holidays and outings, but for every trip there is the inevitable and much dreaded necessity of the long car journey! Sitting in a traffic jam on a hot day with two or three restless children in the back is not many people's idea of fun, but it needn't be the worst part of the day.

The best way to survive the experience is to make it fun. Let the children pack a bag of snacks each, but make sure they don't eat them all at once – the only thing worse than sitting in a traffic jam with bored kids is five hours in a car with a child who's just been sick!

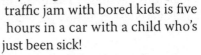

Once you've got your directions sorted out, pass the time with some car games. It really will make the journey seem quicker and should make the experience a lot less stressful for you!

Car Bingo

Before you set off, take some sheets of paper and write or draw a selection of objects for the children to look out for. Choose all the things that they are likely to see on the journey, such as a sheep, a road sign, a lorry and a petrol station, and keep them slightly different for each child. As they see the object, they can tick it off the list. The first to find them all shouts out 'house' and is the winner.

Alternatively, if you have access to the Internet, you will find that there are various websites that have done the work for you already. Just print off the sheets and away you go.

Twenty Questions

One player thinks of an object that falls in the category of either animal, vegetable or mineral, and he/she then tells the other players which of these it is. Everyone else then takes it in turns to ask questions to which the first player can only answer 'yes' or 'no'. If the others do not guess the object when twenty questions have been asked, the first player is the winner. If the object is guessed, the player who gets the correct answer is next to have a go.

For very young children who might not understand the concept of animal, vegetable or mineral, it may be better to limit the game to animals.

Who Am I?

'Who Am I?' is exactly the same as 'Twenty Questions' except that the first player has to think of a famous person, which can be absolutely anyone, from Henry VIII to Madonna. The other players then ask questions such as 'Are you still alive?' and 'Are you male?' and the first to guess the name correctly is the winner.

The Fat Cat Game

This is a surprisingly simple but amusing game. A player thinks of a rhyming adjective and noun, such as 'fat cat' or 'black sack', and then gives a simple clue. The others must then guess the phrase. For example, the clue for 'fat cat' could be 'chubby feline'.

Minister's Cat

This is a classic car game which also encourages younger children to learn their alphabet. Starting at A, each player describes the minister's cat using an adjective beginning with the next letter in the alphabet. So the first player might say 'The minister's cat is an angry cat,' and the next adds another adjective to the phrase, i.e. 'The minister's cat is an angry, black cat.' The phrase gets longer with each letter, and by the time you get to Z, it gets quite tricky to remember them all in the correct order.

Shopping List

Using the same principle as 'Minister's Cat,' this is an alphabetic shopping list. So the first player might say 'I went to the shops and I bought some apples,' and the next could say 'I went to the shops and I bought some apples and some bananas'. So it goes on until all twenty-six letters of the alphabet have been used.

Geography

This game is best for children of seven years and above. The first player names a country and the next must think of another one that begins with the last letter of the previous country. For example, if player one says 'Canada', the next could say 'Australia', and so on. The game carries on until someone is stumped and they are then out. The last person who is still in after everyone can no longer think up new countries is the winner.

Although this is traditionally played with country names, you can adapt it to almost anything. It can be place names, book characters or even pop groups.

Connections

A simple word game that works on quick reactions; one player thinks of a random word and the next person must think of a connecting word as quickly as he can. For example, player one might say 'snow', player two 'cold' and player three 'hot'. Anyone who hesitates, repeats a word that has been said before or chooses an unconnected word is out.

Make Up A Story

Player one starts with a sentence about absolutely anything, for example, 'Johnny was walking through the park when he saw . . .' The next person has to follow on with their own sentence that may or may not be what player one had intended. For example '. . . a one-legged chicken!' It's a great game for encouraging children's imaginations to run wild and is bound to raise some laughs.

Sheep, Horse, Cow

This is an ideal game for pre-school children who might struggle with word games. Each player picks an animal and is given a point when the car passes a field containing those animals. As a point is given, the players switch animals. If you are not driving through countryside, you can pick different coloured cars or lorries for the game.

'Me Time' For Mums: Let's Party!

Even mums are allowed a night out (or a wild night in) occasionally, and when you've been cooped up with the kids all day, there's no better time to let your hair down. So get the glad rags on and make some great cocktails to get you in the mood. Let's party!

Angel's Delight

1¼ fl oz single cream
1 measure triple sec
1 measure gin
2–3 dashes grenadine

Pour the ingredients into a shaker with ice cubes. Shake well and strain into a chilled glass.

*

Tequila Sunrise

2 measures tequila
orange juice
½ measure grenadine
orange slice for garnish
maraschino cherry for garnish

Pour the tequila into a tall glass with ice cubes and add the orange juice until the glass is almost full. Stir. Carefully top the drink with the grenadine so that the colour graduates. Then garnish with the orange and cherry.

White Lady

1 measure gin
½ measure Cointreau
½ measure lemon juice

Pour the ingredients into a shaker with ice cubes. Shake well and strain into a chilled cocktail glass.

White Russian

2 measures vodka
1 measure Kahlúa
¾ fl oz single cream

Pour the vodka and Kahlúa into a tumbler with ice cubes. Stir. Gently top with the cream.

For a Black Russian, leave out the cream.

The joys of motherhood are never fully experienced until the children are in bed.
Author unknown

Sin-free Margarita

This cocktail contains less sugar than the usual margarita, so it has fewer calories. Hurrah!

salt
2 measures tequila
2 tablespoons lime juice, preferably fresh
¼ cup (4 tablespoons) water
¼ teaspoon orange juice
1 tablespoon artificial sweetener liquid or powder

Wet the rim of the glass and dip into a small plate of salt. Combine all the ingredients. You can either serve it over ice, strained into the glass, or mixed in a blender.

Long Island Iced Tea

½ measure triple sec
½ measure light rum
½ measure gin
½ measure vodka
½ measure tequila
1 measure sour mix
cola
lemon wedge for garnish

Pour the spirits and sour mix into a tall glass with ice. Stir well and top the glass off with cola. Garnish with the lemon wedge.

Teen Trouble

OK, so not everything gets easier as the kids get older. Suddenly your sweet little angel turns into a growling, incomprehensible lump who won't move from the sofa. Footballs and Action Man figures give way to smelly socks and acne, and Barbie dolls are ousted for make-up, pop and film star pin-ups.

When you are having the eighteenth row of the day, don't forget that much of it is down to hormones – and who understands those better than a mum? Remember all the mood swings you went through while they were younger, because of pregnancy or PMT? It's payback time!

WHAT YOUR TEENAGER ISN'T TELLING YOU

She's cheerful, helpful and never too far from the phone
She's in love

✳

*He blushes at the mention of a certain name,
or the mere suggestion of a girlfriend*
He's in love

✳

*She's moping around, won't leave the bedroom
and doesn't want to talk to anyone but her friends*
She's been dumped

*He thinks girls are a waste of time
and football/computer games are much better*
He's been dumped

They ask if they can use the landline phone to call a friend
They've overspent on their mobile credit again

✳

*They say, 'I'd rather walk. It's good exercise'
when you offer them a lift*
They're embarrassed to be seen with you or your car

✳

She offers to help you choose a new outfit
She's embarrassed by your clothes

✳

She suggests a girly day out at the shopping centre
She wants some new clothes

*Mother Nature is providential.
She gives us twelve years to develop a love
for our children before turning them into teenagers.*
William Galvin

THINGS YOU SHOULD NEVER SAY TO A TEENAGER IN FRONT OF HIS/HER FRIENDS

Don't you look cute in that?

✻

Make sure you're home by 6 o'clock.

✻

You look just like your dad/mum.

✻

Do you want to dance?

✻

Bring your friends to the karaoke night.
I'm doing a duet with your dad.

✻

Who's my brave little soldier then?

✻

I've got your favourite for tea – alphabetti spaghetti!

✻

You used to have such a cute dimple on your bottom.

✻

You still can't sleep without your teddy, can you darling?

✻

Give me a kiss.

TEEN TALK

Apart from understanding their moods, you also have to negotiate a minefield of language differences. If you find your teenager incomprehensible, here's a little translation for you.

Bovvered – I don't care

＊

Bum – annoying person

＊

Buff – good-looking

＊

Confuzzled – confused

＊

Fit – good looking, attractive

＊

Innit – isn't it (although rarely used in the correct context)

＊

Larry – a person on their own

＊

Minga – an ugly person

＊

Mingin' – horrible or ugly

＊

Toodles – goodbye

＊

Whateva – leave me alone;
I don't want to talk to you; I don't care

TEXT TALK

bt
but

cul8r
see you later

lol
lots of love

Mbr$d
embarrassed

nc
no comment

rUf2t
are you free to talk?

ttyl
talk to you later

:-)
I'm happy

:-(
I'm upset/angry

:) (:
let's meet

YOUTHFUL INDEPENDENCE

Try to think back to when you were a teenager (horrible though that prospect may be). From a teenage point of view, however cool one's parents may be, they are way more embarrassing than anyone else's and will always say and do the wrong thing. And they can't possibly know what their kids are going through!

Always remember that a difficult teen doesn't hate his or her mother; most adolescents are fighting against the world, and their mum is the nearest target!

The hardest thing for a mum to do is to let go. But teenagers need to assert some independence and occasionally (heaven forbid!) make their own mistakes. It's all part of the learning process. The American Academy of Child and Adolescent Psychiatry (AACAP) suggest these golden rules for preparing yourselves, and your teenager, for this difficult period.

✳

Provide a safe and loving home environment.

✳

Create an atmosphere of honesty,
trust and respect.

✳

Allow age-appropriate independence
and assertiveness.

✳

Develop a relationship that encourages your teen
to talk to you when he or she is upset.

Teach responsibility for yours and your teen's belongings.

*

Teach basic responsibility for household chores.

*

Teach the importance of accepting limits.

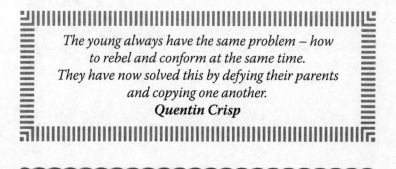

*The young always have the same problem – how
to rebel and conform at the same time.
They have now solved this by defying their parents
and copying one another.*
Quentin Crisp

Mum's Gone Shopping

Shopping is a pastime that universally divides the sexes. Women, on the whole, love it, while men generally hate it. But when a woman decides to go shopping there is one thing she absolutely mustn't take with her – her children!

Unless the purpose of the shopping trip is to buy them clothes and shoes, or they are over the age of fourteen (and female, obviously), they are nothing but a hindrance and their presence will invariably lead to arguments, hair tearing, and, in the worst-case scenario, a very public nervous breakdown.

Tantrums in the aisles, sneaking things into baskets and a constant chorus of 'Mummy, *please* can I have this' is all you can expect if you drag them out, so wait until they are at school, at granny's or at home with dad and ENJOY!

THE SUPERMARKET

Before having children you could hardly imagine that a trip to the local superstore could be a pleasurable experience. When you have tried it with three under-fives you realize the definition of stress-free shopping is a visit to the supermarket *on your own*!

Follow these tips to make your solo trip down the aisles even more of a pleasure.

Tut loudly at every badly behaved child in the store.
You've seen your kids behave like that a million times,
but the poor beleaguered mother dragging her screaming
two-year-old behind her while her four-year-old runs
up and down with the trolley doesn't know that.

✳

Spend hours in the potions and lotions department,
browse in the book section, and look at all the things
you would usually whizz past if you were on a family
shopping trip.

✳

Forget to buy all the cakes and sweets that the children asked
you to bring back and, instead, stock up with exotic fruits
that they have never tried.

✳

Choose a supermarket with a clothes section.
When you get home and moan that groceries are
so expensive these days and that you've just spent £200,
you don't have to mention the two skirts, blouse, handbag
and beautiful leather boots that happened to have fallen
into your trolley!

*The odds of going to the store for a loaf of bread
and coming out with* only *a loaf of bread are
three billion to one.*
Erma Bombeck

> *When women are depressed, they either eat*
> *or go shopping. Men invade another country.*
> *It's a whole different way of thinking.*
> **Elayne Boosler**

CLOTHES SHOPPING

For the ultimate shopping experience, take along a friend (or several) and make a day of it. You can arrange to go somewhere nice for lunch, and you'll have someone to ask 'does my bum look big in this?' Again, it's no good taking the kids. If you try on a fantastic dress for that special occasion, howls of laughter and 'Mummy, you look funny in that' have a tendency to dampen your enthusiasm. Here are some handy hints.

Have an idea what you are looking for. Read magazines or watch a fashion programme before shopping. Shopping for the generic 'new clothes' always ends in disaster.

✳

If you need a skirt, try not to come home with a pair of trousers. As the busy Supermum that you are, another relaxed shopping trip could be a long way off. If you intended to buy one thing, then bought another, it means you will still be longing for the original item as soon as the shopping trip is over.

✳

Try to avoid being diverted into children's departments or toy shops while you're on your shopping spree. Remember that this is *your* time and you must put yourself first for once. Make a note of anything you see for your kids and buy it another time – they'll understand!

✳

Have fun. If you are with friends, try on the most outrageous and unsuitable outfits you can find. The results can be hysterical.

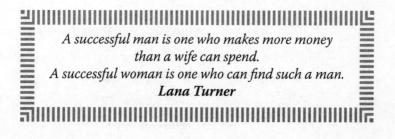

A successful man is one who makes more money than a wife can spend.
A successful woman is one who can find such a man.
Lana Turner

SHOPPING HELL

Even celebrities shop. Let's face it, they have the money. But it's not always a pleasant experience for them.

✳

On a trip to Rome, sex symbol Sophia Loren decided to buy some bras. The well-endowed lady hadn't accounted for the unwanted presence of a rabble of lusty Italian men, and news spread like wildfire. An immense crowd soon gathered in and around the lingerie shop, trapping the actress in her dressing room. It took three fire brigades to break up the riot.

✳

In 2003, airhead heiress Paris Hilton arrived at Las Vegas airport with the fruits of her latest shopping trip in the city and couldn't understand why the flight attendants refused to let her board her plane to Los Angeles. It wasn't surprising when the purchases in dispute were a goat, a monkey and ferret. 'The flight attendants thought I was insane,' recalled Paris. 'They were like, "This isn't a travelling circus – you're not bringing a goat on the plane!"' She managed to get her new pets home eventually, however, after treating them to a six-hour limo ride.

> *Whoever said money can't buy happiness*
> *simply didn't know where to go shopping.*
> ***Bo Derek***

> *Shopping is a woman thing. It's a contact sport like football. Women enjoy the scrimmage, the noisy crowds, the danger of being trampled to death, and the ecstasy of the purchase.*
> **Erma Bombeck**

In 1989, at the age of fourteen, troubled actress Drew Barrymore stole her mother's credit card, flew to Los Angeles, took a variety of drugs, and went to a mall. Some time later, she was asked about her crazy trip. 'What was the point of having a credit card,' she replied, 'if you weren't going to shop!?'

*

Rock star Courtney Love once spent so much money on her credit cards that, when a BMW was fraudulently charged to her, she didn't even notice.

SHOPPERS IN PARADISE

Film director Mark Lewis was proud his mother came from
the Bronx in New York. 'She had a devilish sense of humour,'
he remarked. 'She wanted her ashes spread through
Bloomingdale's when she died. She said she'd bought
a nice cashmere sweater there once. So my brother and I,
we walked around the store spreading her ashes.
It was like that scene when they spread the dirt
from the tunnels around in *The Great Escape*.'

✳

Joan Rivers visited Buckingham Palace in 2002 and headed
straight for the gift shop where she bought dozens of
'God Save The Queen' mugs. 'These,' she explained to staff,
'will be great for all my gay friends!'

✳

During an appearance on Bravo's *Inside the Actor's Studio*
one evening, *Sex and the City* star Sarah Jessica Parker
was asked what sound she loved the most.
She answered, without hesitation, 'Ka-ching!'

COMPULSIVE SHOPPERS

In 2002, actress Salma Hayek admitted that she had been having trouble battling an addiction. 'It was a vice that got completely out of control,' she confessed. It wasn't the usual Hollywood habit of drugs or alcohol, though. It was the Home Shopping Network.

✳

Imelda Marcos, the high priestess of compulsive shoe shopping, once declared: 'I have no weakness for shoes. I wear simple shoes which are pump shoes. It is not one of my weaknesses.' Later, when she fled the Philippines with her husband, she left 3,400 pairs of 'simple' shoes behind!

Actress Dolores Chaplin once remarked that 'Any time I'm depressed, I buy high heels or underwear. That way, at the end of the year, I get a pretty good idea of my psychological state from my wardrobe!'

✳

In 2004, Angelina Jolie visited Macy's in LA. She chose some Ralph Lauren towels and then asked if she could try them out in the changing rooms. 'I need to rub them against my body,' she explained to astonished staff, 'to see if they are soft enough.' Let's hope she ended up buying them . . .

QUEEN OF COUPONS

Susan J. Samtur has made a living out of saving money. Bringing up four sons in New York, on a budget, Susan began to collect coupons to help with the weekly shop. She became so good at this that, in 1973, she and husband Steve launched the magazine *Refundle Bundle,* which now has over two million subscribers.

In 1978, a television reporter accompanied Susan to the supermarket where she stacked her trolley with $130 worth of groceries. When it came to paying for all her goods, Susan presented her coupons and paid the balance – all $7 of it! No doubt the checkout employee was delighted at having to process all those money-off vouchers . . .

It's not easy being a mother.
If it were, fathers would do it.
Dorothy *(from* The Golden Girls*)*

Movie Mums From Hell

Ever had one of those days when you felt like you were the worst mum in the world? The kids have been uncontrollable in the supermarket, you've screamed until you are blue in the face and you've just caught your teenager having a crafty cigarette out of the bedroom window.

If you are in need of reassurance about your parenting skills, settle down with a good film about a bad mother. Cinematic history is littered with examples of bad mothers who make the majority of parents look like Mary Poppins.

Suddenly Last Summer (1959)
'Violet Venables' played by Katherine Hepburn

Violet is the obsessed mother of Sebastian, who died while on holiday with her niece Catherine (Elizabeth Taylor). Her devotion to her dead son is so all-consuming it is sinister and, in order to cover up the nature of Sebastian's death, she tries to have her niece admitted for a lobotomy to rid her of the memory.

Memorable Quote
VIOLET: Oh, Sebastian, what a lovely summer it's been. Just the two of us. Sebastian and Violet. Violet and Sebastian. Just the way it's always going to be. Oh, we are lucky, my darling, to have one another and need no one else ever.

Result
Catherine's doctor refuses to go through with the lobotomy and falls in love with her instead. It turns out Sebastian, a

predatory homosexual, had used his cousin to lure young boys into a trap and a group of them had murdered him in revenge.

The Graduate (1967)
'Mrs Robinson' played by Anne Bancroft

Dustin Hoffman plays Benjamin, a confused twenty-one-year-old, who embarks on an affair with the unhappy wife of his father's business associate. Things are complicated when he falls in love with her sweet daughter, Elaine. When Mrs Robinson finds out she seeks revenge by trying to prevent the two from finding happiness together. The jealous, bitter mum ends up telling her daughter that she never seduced Benjamin, but that he raped her.

Memorable Quotes
MRS ROBINSON: Do you find me undesirable?
BENJAMIN: Oh no, Mrs Robinson. I think, I think you're the most attractive of all my parents' friends. I mean that.

Result
Mrs Robinson fails to get it all her own way, as the besotted Benjamin manages to prevent Elaine from marrying the college boy her parents have chosen. Here's to you, Mrs Robinson.

Carrie (1976)
'Margaret White' played by Piper Laurie

As if social outcast Carrie (Sissy Spacek) didn't have enough to deal with at school, she had to come home to a cruel, religious fanatic of a mother. Beaten and bullied by her evil parent, the worst moment happens when Carrie comes home early from school after enduring the embarrassment of having her first period in front of the girls in gym class. Rather than nurturing and consoling her traumatized daughter, her psycho mum locks her in a closet to do penance for her sins.

Memorable Quote
MARGARET: They're all gonna laugh at you (in response to Carrie's excitement about going to her school Prom Night).

Result
Carrie's rage channels into her powers of telekinesis, and, after having a bucket of pig's blood poured on her head at the Prom, she responds by killing half her classmates. Then she comes home to Mum who also meets a sticky end.

Throw Momma From the Train (1987)
'Mrs Lift' played by Anne Ramsay

Mrs Lift is the domineering mother of the much put-upon Owen (played by Danny DeVito). He wants to have her murdered, but not wishing the trail to lead back to him, he offers to kill the troublesome ex of a lecturer, Larry (Billy Crystal), in return for the disposal of his own mum.

Memorable Quote

MOMMA: Owen! Food!

OWEN: In a minute, Momma.

MOMMA: Don't you 'In a minute, Momma' me! Get off your fat little ass or I'll break it for you! I want two soft-boiled eggs, white toast, and some of that grape jelly, God damn it! And don't burn the toast!

OWEN: Kill her, Larry.

Result

Owen repeatedly badgers Larry to kill 'Momma' but, finally, when Larry agrees, the Mummy's boy backs down and decides he doesn't want her dead after all.

The Grifters (1990)
'Lilly Dillon' played by Anjelica Huston

Two-bit con artist Roy Dillon (played by John Cusack) is trying to build a loving relationship with his hard-hearted mother. Seeing him as a threat, she keeps him at arm's length and constantly puts him down.

Memorable Quote

ROY: I guess I owe you my life, Lilly.

LILLY: You always did, Roy.

Result

After an elaborate scam, Lilly and Roy fight over a briefcase full of money. When the glass that Roy is holding breaks and stabs him in the jugular, he dies in a pool of blood. Lilly is naturally a little upset, but manages to get over her grief long enough to snatch the case and take off into the sunset.

Wild at Heart (1990)
'Marietta Fortune' played by Diane Ladd

The mother of Laura Dern, both on- and off-screen, Diane played Marietta as a possessive witch-like character who would do anything to keep her daughter away from her lover, Sailor, and is constantly trying to have him killed. As if that's not bad enough, it turns out her murderous intent is not prompted by a desire to protect her daughter, but by her own feelings of rejection after Sailor rebuffed her advances.

Memorable Quote
Most of what she said was X-rated and unprintable!

Result
Lula and Sailor hit the road and embark on a crime spree, while Marietta has a breakdown.

Serial Mom (1993)
'Beverly R. Sutphin' played by Kathleen Turner

On the surface, the Sutphins are the perfect suburban family, but Beverly takes her protective instinct a little further than most. Perceived slights against her family result in obscene phone calls to the neighbours and a mounting body count.

Memorable Quote
MISTY: He killed people, mom.
BEVERLY: We all have our bad days.

Result
The domestic goddess-turned-murderess is finally tracked down by the police and the nuclear family goes into meltdown.

The Manchurian Candidate (2003)
'Eleanor Shaw' played by Meryl Streep

In the remake of the original 1962 film, Meryl Streep plays a power-hungry senator who will stop at nothing. When her son, Raymond Shaw (played by Liev Schrieber), is hailed as a war hero, it kickstarts his political career and helps him on his way to become a vice presidential candidate. But an ex-army colleague begins to realize that the entire unit were kidnapped and brainwashed, and the trail leads back to domineering mother Senator Shaw.

Memorable Quote
ELEANOR: The assassin always dies, baby. It's necessary for the national healing.

Result
By her own design, her son is programmed to become an assassin, and she orders him to kill another politician, Senator Jordon. He shoots both the Senator and his daughter, who, in a twist of fate, is the woman with whom he's in love. Eventually Raymond and his mother get their comeuppance when ex-Captain Marco, one of the brainwashed soldiers, kills them both.

Other Mums' Books
(to be read after this one!)

Grumpy Old Women
by Judith Holder

A hilarious collection of thoughts from famous grumpy old women including Janet Street-Porter, Jenny Eclair, Ann Widdecombe, Germaine Greer and Jilly Cooper.

✳

Ask Your Mother
by Ruth Carpenter

Subtitled '50 Things You Should Have Learnt from Your Mother, But Probably Didn't', it has tips on everything from putting on lipstick to unblocking a sink.

✳

Confessions of a Failed Grown-up:
Bad Motherhood & Beyond
by Stephanie Calman

The witty insights of a mother who has never felt ready to be one. Stephanie struggles to cope with the expectations of how mothers should behave and fails to be perfect – like most of us.

Memoirs of an Unfit Mother
by Anne Robinson

Written by journalist and presenter Anne Robinson, this is a brutally honest look at her relationship with her mother and, subsequently, her daughter. A hugely successful Fleet Street journalist, Anne lost custody of her daughter in a bitter divorce and then faced a long battle against alcohol addiction. A brave and inspirational book.

✳

Minus Nine to One:
The Diary of an Honest Mum
by Jools Oliver

Jamie Oliver's wife has always wanted to be a mum, but the experiences of pregnancy and birth brought plenty of unexpected surprises. A funny look at the highs and lows of being a new mum.

✳

Mother, Missing
by Joyce Carol Oates

A touching account of a grown-up daughter coming to terms with the sudden loss of her mother.

✳

The Ninth Life of Louis Drax
by Liz Jensen

One of the most moving and compelling novels ever written about the relationship between a mother and son. Seen through the eyes of a boy in a coma and his doctor, you won't be able to put it down.

Things You Wish Your Mother Had Told You

Babies always wait until you have taken their nappy off to pee.

✳

Men never buy tasteful underwear.

✳

Most desserts are just as good if they're shop bought. Remember: 'Stressed' is 'Desserts' spelled backwards.

✳

Lunching with your friends constitutes childcare, as long as they have children too.

✳

It always rains at school pick-up time.

If men man the barbecue, they must receive ALL the praise – even if you've spent all morning in the kitchen preparing the salad and side dishes.

✳

You can't argue with a five-year-old without sounding like one yourself.

✳

When a baby is awake, you want him to be asleep, and when he's asleep you want him awake. Conversely, when a teenager is at home, you want him to go out. When he's out, you want him back in the house.

✳

Life's too short to bake a cake.

✳

If you have children of your own, you will inevitably end up sounding just like your mother!

The Joke's On Mum

Little Johnny had finished his summer holiday and returned to school. Two days later his teacher phoned his mother to tell her that her son was misbehaving.

'Wait a minute,' said his mother. 'I had Johnny with me for three months and I never called you once when he misbehaved.'

A man passed a woman in the supermarket with a three-year-old girl in her trolley. As they passed the biscuit section, the child asked for some, but her mother told her 'No'. The little girl immediately began to cry, and the mother said, 'Now Lucy, we just have half of the aisles left to get through, don't be upset. It won't be long.'

He passed the mother again beside the sweets counter. The little girl began to shout for chocolate and once again was told

'No', so she started to cry. Patiently, the mother said, 'There, there, Lucy, don't cry. Only two more aisles to go, and then we'll be going to the checkout.'

At the checkout, Lucy wanted a lolly, and thwarted for a third time, she started to bawl even louder. 'Lucy, we'll be finished in five minutes, and then you can go home and have a nice nap', the mother said.

As they left, the man stopped the woman to compliment her. 'I couldn't help noticing how patient you were with little Lucy', he remarked.

The mother replied, 'My little girl's name is Jenny. I'm Lucy!'

✳

What the difference between a Jewish mother and a Rottweiler?

A Rottweiler eventually lets go.

✳

An exasperated mother, whose son was always getting into mischief, finally asked him, 'How do you expect to get into Heaven?'

The boy thought it over and said, 'Well, I'll just run in and out and in and out and keep slamming the door until St Peter says, "For Heaven's sake, Jimmy, come in or stay out!"'

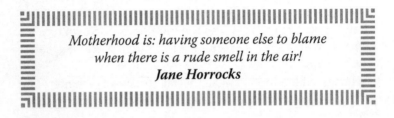

Motherhood is: having someone else to blame when there is a rude smell in the air!
Jane Horrocks